When the Angels Come Calling

Tony Cooper

I am not seeking to profit from this book, my motive is to use any revenues to support my 1st choice charity 'Fight Bladder Cancer'. It's such a horrible disease, not only in the context of taking lives but also for the misery that it dishes out along the way. Even though it's the 4th or 5th most common form of cancer it lacks the resources and publicity of others, namely breast and prostate, and is hugely underfunded by comparison.

So, I appeal to each of you and ask if you would make a further, small donation to this wonderful charity. Of course there are so many worthwhile causes that we all support and it can be difficult to make distinctions, but this is one that I hold dear to my heart and they really do need help.

Donations can be made at:
www.fightbladdercancer.co.uk

If your generosity helps save even one life then our collective effort has been so worthwhile.

ACKNOWLEDGEMENTS

1. First and foremost my wife **Judy**, but not just for the moral support she has given through the past year. I knew she could draw a little and so I asked if she would provide some illustrations. I wasn't at all prepared for what I got. Her work is outstanding, much of which is of such high quality that I think she should turn professional! She really has put the icing on the cake, thank you so much.

2. 'North Stand Chat', a forum for Brighton and Hove Albion supporters has been a limitless resource for just about anything. It is one of the most, if not <u>the</u> most, active football forums in the country with around 25,000 members. If ever I needed anything I could go there and find it. I have had builders, plumbers, decorators and I was even introduced to my accountant through the forum. I use it to get restaurant, TV and movie recommendations, holiday ideas and advice on which TV, phone or laptop to buy. It is so much more than a football forum with topics on just abut anything from football, to bird watching, current affairs to gardening etc, you name it and you'll find a discussion on it. I knew if I needed help with my book I would find it there, and I did. Huge thanks to <u>**John Challon**</u> (AKA Greg Bobkin) for helping me with the task of editing and cleaning the whole mess up. Unwittingly he got me over the line, when I came across him I was only about 75% of the way through, but his just being there and engaging helped and gave me the kick I needed.

3. My Pal **Paul Singer**, a friend of 40 years and one time (almost) business partner, none of which gets mentioned in this book and which made me realise I could write another complete book and still have more to say. But huge thanks for the photoshop work and sorting my eyes out! Couldn't and wouldn't have done it without you.

4. Finally **Derek Hall** for his brilliant typesetting. I didn't even appreciate that I needed it but he has put this book together wonderfully and I am most grateful. I have rarely come across anyone with such extreme patience and he hand held me through every step of the process. Goodness knows how he put up with my tardiness!

PREFACE

For years, many people have encouraged me to write a book, I'd not given it a second thought until recently. But, after a little bit of bullying by some of my friends – and realising my time on this earth is unfortunately drawing to a close – I thought I should at least give it a try!

I think those who encouraged me expect this book to be a rib-tickling and amusing reflection of my life – and I hope much of it is. But the truth is that there have been sad moments, and others that I am not so proud of. I managed to find a good coping mechanism to deal with some of the downs, but acknowledge that I was never totally successful in dealing with some of the demons that haunted me. I will do my utmost to complete this account of my life truthfully and hopefully it will entertain you, even if you don't know me.

This is very much a factual account of my life. Anything that might not be fact is either my memory failing, or 'embellished' to protect my dignity or the dignity of others.

Despite some downs, most of the past 60+ years have been ups and I simply couldn't contemplate the thought of trading my life for anyone else's even in this dark period. Not only have I lived a full, rich, enjoyable life – supported for the most part by a (relatively) highly successful career – but to change anything would likely mean my two lovely girls, Fran (not Frankie!) and Steph, would not be a product of my life. Nor would I have had the opportunity to spend such precious, but too short, time with my lovely wife Judy whom I adore so much more than she will ever know. That she might not really know is a reflection of my own emotional reluctance which even now, I am still trying to overcome.

I dedicate this book to the exceptionally wonderful Judy who has been not only a rock at my side throughout the past 15 or so years, but also unquestionably my very best mate. I am truly humbled.

Also to my loyal and caring daughters who I have tried so hard to raise with the right values and to steer along the right path, to avoid making some of the mistakes that I did.

And finally, my special friends who have enriched my life, stood beside me through thick and thin and who I hope will read my story with a smile on their face and warmth in their hearts. I hope they can take some satisfaction in knowing that I always regarded all of them as 'Premier League Mates' ... they know who they are!

My heartfelt thanks to you all x

CONTENTS

1 - THE PENULTIMATE CHAPTER

I know exactly when it started. Well, not started, but let's say showed it's ugly face. It was September 7th, 2021 and Judy and I had arranged to meet Harty at a golf driving range near Leatherhead to hit a bucket of balls and play a six-hole round of golf. I played golf regularly with Harty when we were both working at American Express in the late 80's – he was an accomplished golfer and great fun to play with. But once he became a father, he eased back on golf and, given his love of sailing, decided to spend more time on the water than the fairway. Anyway, I had been badgering him for about 10 years (when he'd sold his last yacht) to get back into golf and when he did, I was delighted.

I was equally happy that Judy had decided to take up golf and, being naturally athletic with good hand/eye coordination, I was in no doubt she would turn into a very capable golfer. That September day was a combination of a couple of firsts. It was the first time Judy had been on a golf course and also the first time (as I recall) that Harty had used his brand new set of shiny TaylorMade clubs in which he had invested £2,000 (or £700 if you were his wife, Sarah).

It was a hot day, very hot! We spent a good 45 minutes on the range hitting ball after ball and weighing up all the statistics that are now presented via the very sophisticated technology: distance of travel; spin speed; angle of trajectory, etc, etc. All were of little use to a golfer of my standard, but we were fully loosened up and ready to attack the course. The next hour was a complete waste of time and not worthy of comment. Judy had buggered her wrist up, I lost interest as soon as I sliced my first drive way over the car park and Harty just went about his business in his normal calm and consistent way. It was scorchio hot and I knew we hadn't taken on enough liquid, but we were finishing our round and the clubhouse was waiting. However, before we could get a drink, Harty had a call from Sarah to say their Westie doggy needed an urgent trip to the vet and he had to leave. So I suggested (I rarely *'suggest'* anything by the way) to Judy that rather than go in the clubhouse we might stop on the way home for lunch somewhere. We set off but along the way we agreed (I do *'agreement'* quite well) that we should just head home and have lunch there.

After lunch I went for a wee and was quite shocked to

see it was a reddy brown or dark rusty colour. Judy, who is far smarter than I at anything in the medical department, said I was likely dehydrated so, over the course of the next few hours, I consumed several large glasses of water. By bedtime my wee had returned to a more normal colour, phew!

Three days later – September 10th, was my 67th birthday and arriving to spend the night before we all went on holiday together were Stewart and Ellen and Phil and Ceris. I had known both couples since I joined their company 30 years earlier. We had a nice evening out ahead of catching the ferry from Newhaven the next morning, en route to Dieppe and onward to Saumur in the Loire Valley. The ferry journey was pleasant, relaxing and uneventful – until I needed to go for a wee. This time it wasn't just rusty, it was very deep red. Indeed, it was so obviously wrong that the chap in the next bay to me uttered a loud expletive and nearly fainted. I looked at what he was looking at and went into mild shock, rooted to the spot. I returned to the group and managed to hook Judy away and give her the news. "More water, you must drink more water", she said. And so I spent the remainder of the journey drinking copious amounts of water (something that seemingly didn't go unnoticed).

Over the course of the remainder of that day and evening, the colour became less dramatically wrong but still far from right. I didn't sleep well and so the next morning (my eldest daughter, Francesca's birthday) we left a note for the others giving them a little detail and that I needed to get to a hospital and headed off into Saumur. Now, my experience of hospitals is virtually nil. I'd been in twice, for the birth of each of my daughters and a further time when my youngest, Stephanie, had suffered with a short period of seizures as a two-year-old. So I didn't really know what to expect, plus it was France! However, I was so pleasantly surprised to be well looked after by extremely understanding staff. Samples were taken and, once done, we waited for about 90 minutes for results. A very nice doctor explained that I had an infection, for which he provided a prescription for 14 days of antibiotics. But he added that I needed to see a urology specialist for more tests on what was causing the issue as he had concerns. He gave me a letter (primarily for my own doctor) confirming everything.

I tried hard not to let any of this impact on our holiday and the enjoyment of others, which was generally successful. Conversely, trying to get any sense out of my GP practice at home when I called them the day after visiting hospital, was impossible. I said I would return immediately if it were considered necessary, but the front line telephone staff refused to pass any message on to my doctor, saying I had to make an appointment when I got back. They would not allow me to make an appointment as they only took appointments on the day and so I was forced to wait until we returned home.

I'll digress here and say that, despite my condition, we

had a wonderful holiday in the most delightful location with great friends. Rural France just cannot be beaten in my view. Wherever you go it's consistently peaceful, romantic and, well, just classy. The food is to die for (not a Pizza Express, Nando's, Frankie and Benny's or such like to be seen!) the countryside dramatically serene and the hospitality first class. I love it and I regret that I didn't get to treat Judy to more of it.

Once back home, I tried unsuccessfully to see my GP (by the time I got through to make an 'on the day' appointment, they had all gone) and it was a week before I 'saw' her (it was actually on the phone). She asked for a wee sample, which, after her analysis, led her to the conclusion I had an infection and I was prescribed another seven days antibiotics. At the end of that course, I still had traces of x, y and z in my wee and so she finally referred me to the Urology department of my local hospital - hooray!

I showed up at hospital to be greeted by a lovely specialist urology nurse who, for some reason was holding what appeared to be a fishing rod. She asked me to remove my trousers and pants and then told me the fishing rod is actually a camera and that she was going to insert it into my bladder, through the shortest route. At this point I decided I didn't need any more attention and, if we left now, we could be home for lunch. Judy refused to allow it and said camera was sent up my innards. The (now less lovely) nurse asked if I wanted to look at the picture on her screen. I declined. She then announced that there was a golf ball-sized tumour in my bladder, which would require surgery to remove. I don't actually remember much else about that day, somehow we got home in one piece.

Less than two weeks later, I was in hospital being operated on. The second worst thing about my 36 hours in hospital was the food, which was excruciatingly bad. So much so that for my last meal I ordered a cheese sandwich in the knowledge that there was little that could go wrong. How they got it so badly wrong was bewildering, but I concluded that whoever was responsible for what was put in front of me had intended it to go to a prison, or maybe a pig farm! The bread was not only stale but tasted of salt. It wasn't buttered and the cheese (about four pieces the size of postage stamps) was entirely tasteless and rock hard.

I felt no discomfort from the surgery, but I did from a catheter that had been put in during the procedure. I actually had one the week before as my bladder wasn't emptying correctly and I can assure you that it is not a bit of kit I would recommend. Essentially, a mini hosepipe put where the fishing rod was put two weeks earlier and out to a bag strapped to my leg with a drain tap on the bottom. I was told that if I could wee OK, then I could be discharged 'catheterless' and this intrusive medieval torture device was removed (not without discomfort too). I spent the rest of the day pacing up and down the ward with plastic bucket in hand and made regular trips to the water station and toilet. Unfortunately, I was unsuccessful and later in the day I was told I had to leave with the device back in. I think the nurse was at the end of his shift because I had no sooner protested/appealed than I was on my back with the hosepipe being re-inserted. Deep joy.

Over the course of the next two weeks I suffered more than one embarrassing moment, including leaving a large puddle in an very fancy restaurant in Lewes and leaving a trail behind me on an afternoon walk through town. Dignified it most certainly wasn't!

I returned to hospital two weeks later for a TWOC (Trial without Catheter) – another pleasant experience! Basically, the nurse pumped water into my bladder through a valve on the torture equipment and asked me to count from one to 10 as I felt my bladder filling – 1 being empty and 10 absolutely bursting. She was going to disconnect at 8. I did as I was told and then she removed the equipment. I was free again and boy did it feel good. She then gave me a jug and said 'wee'. I couldn't. This led to me spending the rest of the day in hospital, walking over 20,000 steps to try and get some action, but failing. I was then given the option of DIY torture, meaning whenever I couldn't go I had to torture myself, (sorry about all this – it was supposed to be a fun book!) or they would put the permanent catheter back. I opted for the former. I won't bore you with the details but, as I write, even though my bladder has partially recovered I have to go through this routine two or three times a day. I'm actually becoming quite accomplished at it and can even do it with my eyes closed.

A day or two later I returned to hospital to meet the consultant urologist, a very nice man but with a very nasty message. The cancer was very aggressive, had spread beyond the bladder wall and there was evidence (from an earlier scan) that it had reached distant lymph nodes and my condition was terminal. They could do nothing for me. I was getting tired of this bad news but, I think I was expecting it. Judy was brave, but extremely distressed. I did my best to console her, because my concern was immediately for her, as it has been ever since getting that dreadful news.

Further visits resulted in me going into a 18-week programme of chemotherapy. After that, I would have to endure immunotherapy the (same as chemotherapy but a different drug) every two weeks for the rest of my life – well, until the immunotherapy drug became ineffective. None of the medication is going to change the prognosis, but it might buy us a little extra time.

By December 2021, I was in isolation (with Judy) because Covid was rampant and I had no defence against it, or indeed against any kind of virus or infection. During that time, I started to 'help' (train) Judy in all the aspects of work that I did in our day-to-day lives: finances; car; ironing; everything she needed to know how to do in life after me. Neither of us really appreciated just how much I did, I was impressed with myself and also impressed by her brilliance in picking up these things.

One thing I must say is that those days were my first

real interactions with the doctors and nurses of the NHS and I was blown away by the care, attention, concern and dedication of everyone that I interacted with. I can't find the words to express my total respect or thanks and I think they all deserve medals and huge recognition. They really should never be taken for granted.

With all that now explained, I can get on and tell you a little bit about my life and its many ups and downs.

2 - CREEPY CRAWLEY

If you've never been to Crawley, my advice is don't – you're really not missing much! It used to be called an overspill town, but someone decided that didn't sound very nice, so it got changed to 'New Town'. The rebrand didn't disguise the fact that it is a series of estates planned by someone with zero imagination and who had obviously spent too much time in a Gulag. Much of the housing was just functional and hugely uninspiring – and each estate had its own countrified sounding name, such as Pound Hill, Tilgate and Gossops Green. OK, forget the countrified but it might have been an idea.

Number 11 Maiden Lane, Langley Green was a typical three-bed (end) terrace council house and where I lived with my Dad, Mum and elder (half) sister Gaby. She was 10 years older than me and by the time I was starting to understand stuff and how life worked she was planning her escape to a more salubrious address in Furnace Green.

My Dad died when I was just five years old and, although I can picture him vividly, I have very little recollection of anything else. In saying that, there were two occasions that have stuck with me. He was a keen gardener and I remember one day I was in the garden with him while he was boiling up a huge pot of soil. Seemingly, by doing so, it killed off the bad stuff and improved the good stuff. Anyway, he or I knocked the pot and the contents went all over my shoulder. I vaguely remember being taken to hospital by ambulance but not much else. It left me with scars, that I still have now.

The second occasion was driving back from my grandfather's in Bognor. We stopped at the top of Bury Hill (a very steep hill about a mile long) where my Dad said he could get some really good soil for the garden. Off he went with his spade and two sacks. He returned about 10-15 minutes later with a sack on each shoulder and put them into the back of the car. He looked exhausted and the weight of the sacks had clearly had an impact and my mother told him off! We set off for home, but within 100 yards he slumped over the steering wheel. It was scary and also, because the hill was so steep, the car was picking up speed. Somehow, goodness knows how, my mother was able to lean across and steer us to safety, despite being unable to reach any of the pedals, we eventually get to the bottom of the hill and the car rolls to a stop outside a pub (you really can't make this stuff up). My Dad came round a little and my mother got help from the pub and took him inside. I remember being taken into the publicans' living area and left alone for an eternity. It must have been a long time because the next thing I knew I was asleep in bed at home.

When I got up and went downstairs my mother sat me down and told me my dad had died. He was 48.

I don't think I was even old enough to comprehend what that meant - either that or I went into some sort of childlike state of shock. Whichever it was, the impact of his passing took several months to really hit home.

After that, life seemed fairly normal for a kid of my age, but it was only as I grew up that I realised just how far from normal it really was. I began to appreciate that I was little more than a burden to my mother. She fed and clothed me but I didn't get much else from her. No unconditional love that comes with a parent/child relationship and certainly no parental guidance whatsoever. Despite that I enjoyed my time at primary school, I had lots of friends and two, in particular, stick in my mind. The first one was my best friend, Ricky Buglass. His Mum was German and used to sunbathe topless in their back garden so, on warm sunny days, Ricky was everyone's best mate and we would all dash to his house after school. The second friend was Colin, who lived three or four doors down from us. I used to go to Colin's house for tea quite often - his Mum was really nice and I remember thinking I would like her to be my Mum. Part of the reason Colin stuck in my mind was because he had a strange habit of eating his food one ingredient at a time.

Nobody ever came to our house for tea.

I never really worked out my Mum, mostly because I didn't want to. In fact, it wasn't long before I began to think of her as an embarrassment. I know she was born into a very affluent family but there aren't too many other things I know about her, only bits based on how she portrayed herself. I do know her father was the youngest ever stockbroker with his own firm in the City of London. And that she was educated at St Paul's and went to finishing school in Geneva. She owned one or more racehorses. She skied in St Moritz with Fred Perry. She was a Cordon Bleu-trained chef and was taught music by Gustav Holst. Whilst I can't evidence any of that I can confirm that she smoked like a trooper, drank like a fish and was totally reckless with money. But, out of respect (misplaced perhaps) that she was my mother, I'll not tell you about the really bad stuff. She had no money whatsoever and life growing up was not only without a father and an all but absent mother, but also one without too many treats or positive experiences.

I was essentially an only child. My (half) sister left home when I was about seven and my three elder (half) brothers had all left home before I had ever really met them. Indeed, two of them were raised in an orphanage – even now I still don't really know why – and the other was raised in France by his French father. The first time I met him he couldn't speak English.

In those days we had an exam called 11+, a blunt instrument to segregate kids for their secondary education. Pass and you go to Grammar school; fail and you go to 'Secondary Modern', as they were known. I passed and then my Mum decided that I should go to a top educational establishment – difficult when paying next week's rent was always a challenge. Not only did she want me to have a good education (very out of character that she should care) but she also wanted me to board (very much in character) and I was accepted into two schools: Christ's Hospital near Horsham and The Royal Hospital School near Ipswich. Now, the fees for these schools (today) are in the region of £35,000 a year, which meant a tricky situation for a woman who didn't have a pot to **** in.

But she was a very tenacious and persuasive woman. I remember my very first trip to London – actually I think it was my very first trip anywhere apart from a Sunday school outing to Brighton. I was meeting with some bigwig from Bovis construction to be interviewed with a view to the company funding my entire education at Christ's Hospital in exchange for me joining the business once my education was completed. I remember gawping at this huge office building near Hyde Park corner and we were taken up in the lift to the top floor and introduced to Mr Bovis (or whatever his name was). He said hello to me and then spoke double dutch to my Mum while I spent the time looking out of the window and taking in all the sights. They were quite something for someone who was only used to their school, the local park, Dr Johnson pub and Bests newsagents. 'Mr Bovis' then turned his attention to me and handed me a foolscap (A4 in new money) pad and a pencil and told me to write a 1,000 word statement on what I was thinking while I came up in the lift. I was 10 years old! Even now I have no idea what I wrote and I probably made it all up anyway, because in my experience a typical 10-year-old boy thinks of not very much at all most of the time.

After the interview my mum treated me to lunch at an Italian restaurant (who said she didn't care?). When we had finished, the waiter brought the bill and she simply refused to pay it saying the food wasn't to her liking and she dragged me out and down Oxford Street with the waiter chasing and shouting at us. She was not in the least bit interested in his protestations and he eventually gave up his pursuit.

Shortly after the Bovis interview we heard that I had been successful and they would fund my entire education at Christ's Hospital. My Mum had also managed to persuade a charity for the children of former naval servicemen (my Dad was in the Royal Marines for many years) to fund my fees at The Royal Hospital School. I chose The Royal Hospital School because the boys at Christ's Hospital had to wear skirts and I thought it was effeminate (actually, I was only 10 so I thought it was plain silly). I also have a vague recollection that I chose it because it was further away from home.

So that was Creepy Crawley. As you can see, apart from the sight of Ricky's Mum sunbathing there weren't too many positive experiences.

There were, however, some very negative experiences that I have had to fight against all my life. Not long after my Dad died I was molested, more than once I think, by a close family member. Something that, at the time, I didn't realise was even wrong, so young was I. I knew I didn't like it, though. I have no idea how or even why I bottled it up right through until I was in my early 60s. I get why, as a youngster, I might have been frightened, but once I was of an age when I really understood what had happened to me, it's a mystery why I stayed quiet. Even worse, not only did I keep it a secret for most of my life, but I never said anything at all to the perpetrator and allowed him to have a perfectly normal relationship with me. I don't know what eventually made me open up, but I did – to Judy. I think the love I knew she had for me and my love for her gave me the confidence and it was such a relief to get it all out in the open. I should have done it many years earlier for it has blighted many aspects of my life. I subsequently told the perpetrator (by email) that I never wanted to see him or hear from him again. Deep down I wanted, expected even, an apology, but none came. However, I felt a huge weight had been lifted from me, somehow the demons had been exorcised and I could get on with my life, or what was left of it.

I intended to name the person here but have chosen not to, for no other reason than to protect the feelings and dignity of his children.

3 - SCHOOL DAYS

I thoroughly enjoyed my time at The Royal Hospital School. It has a wonderful history - established in 1712, it moved from Greenwich (the buildings are now the national maritime museum) to near Ipswich in 1933. The school was originally established to provide education to underprivileged children from seafaring backgrounds and, in 1964, when I first attended it still had a very strong naval presence. For example, our school uniforms were various elements of Royal Navy uniform right up to the full dress, which was worn for special events. The school was set on over 200 acres and had numerous football, rugby and cricket pitches as well as several tennis courts and an Olympic size swimming pool. I was in heaven.

I boarded, of course, and I was put into Howe House. Each house accommodated about 50 boys (it wasn't until much later that it became a co-ed school) and there were 12 houses in total, all named after a famous naval Admiral. We were housed in dormitories of about 12, while the senior boys had their own small rooms.

The education was first-class, but it was the sport that really excited me and we had loads of time to practice and participate in a variety of sports. I soon found myself in the school first team for football, second team for rugby and also represented the school in cross country, freestyle swimming and middle distance athletics. I made lots of good friends but, sadly, have lost touch with all of them.

Quite often, I would stay at school for half term. My Mother moved to Southend shortly after I started there and, as I knew nobody in that place, there seemed little point going home. Lots of other kids stayed over too, mostly those whose parents lived overseas, so there was always plenty to do and other boys for company.

I remember my Mum visiting the school, but only once - and that was an end of term Speech Day where there was lots of pomp and ceremony. I also recall that the then Prime Minister, Jim Callaghan, was the guest VIP and gave the speech.

My Mum married the lodger she had in Southend, Spirodian Constantine Anthony Petropulo (but I called him Pete the Greek). He would have been in his mid 50s and worked in a fairly mundane job at a shipping company somewhere in the City. Shortly after they married, the two of them moved to Haywards Heath, into a nice council flat that was a two-minute walk from the town centre. He was a decent chap and, after a difficult period adjusting to the fact that I had a 'new Dad', we got on well. He looked after my Mum and my relationship with him was good.

As I went through my early senior school years I quickly decided that I wanted to be a military helicopter pilot, mostly influenced by the heritage of the school. But also, there was a lot of news about the Vietnam war at the time and much of it involved helicopters – to a 12/13-year-old boy it all appeared very adventurous. I wasn't very keen on naval flying as the sea didn't appeal, so I decided I would join the Army Air Corps when the time came. To get in, I would need three A levels and I was confident that would not be an issue as I was doing extremely well academically.

By the time I reached the 4th year (Year 10 now) I was getting really fed up going home on school holidays and knowing nobody. At 15, having just your Mum and Stepdad as your social network for up to eight weeks does nothing for your street cred. Therefore I made the decision to leave the Royal Hospital School and go to the local Grammar school. I'll never know how that impacted my life, but I suspect it was one of those life changing decisions that one makes and I might have got completely wrong. I reflected later in life that my Mum did absolutely nothing to stop me leaving, which puzzled me a lot as she always had an opinion and although never proactive she was brilliant at reactive stuff.

We applied to the Grammar school but, despite me flying through all their entrance testing I was rejected because I had not studied Latin. I was joining a year that had another two terms to go before pupils could drop the subject ahead of their GCE's. It was an absurd system, but one that was totally rigid and I was therefore packed off to the local comprehensive. Now, bearing in mind where I had come from, this was like going into a war zone. Although top streamed in every subject, I could not insulate myself from the general school population much of which had zero interest in education and quite a lot of interest in such things as the opposite sex (completely alien to me) fashion and apparel (what, no uniform?) fighting, shoplifting and various acts of vandalism. I'm not sure how long it was before I wondered how big a mistake I had made, leaving my nice, posh, civilised school, it could be measured in days though.

At first I was bullied quite badly but I learnt to fight back and, once I did, the bullies gave up on me. I made a few friends principally by getting into the school football and athletics teams (they didn't play rugby or have a swim team unfortunately). But I was never happy at this school. The education was dreadful – more to do with disruptive children than poor teaching standards – and adapting to the new environment was very tough indeed.

I really enjoyed my football and got to play for the town's youth team as a pretty capable inside left (No 10 nowadays). We would get regular visits from Brighton scouts, but I never impressed enough to get called for trials. One of my best friends, John Parsons – a brick shithouse of a centre back - did but sadly he never made the grade. It was during this period that I became an avid Brighton and Hove Albion fan and would get to most home games at the old and dilapidated Goldstone Ground, squirming my way into the middle of a packed North Stand. The team were, for the most part, in one of the bottom two leagues but I did get to watch a few seasons in the second tier.

It was very noticeable that John was doing very well for himself in other areas. Several of us would cycle to school and one day he appeared with a spankingly posh 10-gear Claude Butler racer. We'd already noticed he was wearing top of the range trainers, jeans and other stuff and I thought it was odd, given he came from a very working class background. Everyone was intrigued and he explained to us that he had a new job one evening a week and Saturdays gardening for a very wealthy lady in one of the best parts of town (Fox Hill). We all pleaded with him to get us a job there too, but it fell on deaf ears. That was until one day, when he took pity on me and said he had got me four hours working alongside him on Saturday afternoons. He explained that the lady was a bit odd, (he actually should have said 'totally barking mad').

On my first day we duly arrived at a very grand, but badly maintained, house and the first thing I noticed was that the gardens were a mess. It certainly wasn't what I expected from a lad who was doing 10-12 hours a week looking after them. We knocked on the front door and, after an eternity, an old lady opened it. Although John had prepared me, I wasn't REALLY prepared. We were greeted by a woman who, to this 14/15-year-old, looked abut 200 years old. In fact, she didn't look like any woman I had ever seen, the long dark beard had me fixated. The other immediately noticeable thing was the smell. It absolutely stank and, looking beyond the lady (Mrs Bostock), the reason was obvious: there was dog mess all over the place. We were invited in, I held back but John shoved me though the door and we followed her into the living room. There were no carpets anywhere downstairs and the living room contained only a big leather armchair at the side of which was a pint mug and a near empty bottle of brandy and a big television. That was it. Dog poo had been deposited liberally throughout! I don't recall what was said as I was totally focussed on holding back my desire to wretch.

Thankfully we escaped before I was actually sick. We went to the back of the garden and sat in the shed talking abut football, fishing, girls and whatever else kids of our age talked about for the next couple of hours. The one thing we didn't do was any gardening. We then went back into the house (I really didn't want to but John insisted) and he told Mrs Bostock we were done. She asked how much she owed and he said £25 for him and £15 for me. Now, this was in about 1969/70 and I think in today's money it would be about £150 and £100 respectively. So I'd just been paid about a year of pocket money for two hours of doing nothing! But more was to come. Mrs Bostock asked John to get her a dozen bottles of brandy and asked how much they were, he replied £5 each and she went into her purse and got out £75 and gave it to him. I nearly fainted (shock, smell or both, who knows?). I don't know how much of that I got – probably half – but regardless, it was more money than I had ever seen.

That routine continued for many weeks/months. John explained that the lady's son (a high-ranking Army officer) had told him that if she ever asked for brandy John should agree to get it but not to buy it, as the son was regulating her consumption. If John's story was true, then I don't think he ever mentioned to the son how much money was being passed over – otherwise it surely would've been stopped. Anyway, the paying out of huge amounts of money continued for several months until one day John came to school and told us that when he visited the previous evening, Mrs Bostock attacked him with an axe. Her dog had died and she thought John had poisoned it. Seemingly, she was then committed to an institution. Goodness knows how much money I had accumulated, but it felt like a small fortune for a schoolboy and, naturally, I could not tell my Mum. So, not being the thrifty sort, I spent it all on a very posh racing bike, loads of new top end sea fishing equipment (Les Moncrieff beach casters and Penn multiplier reels). My Mum did enquire as to where I was getting the money from and I 'fibbed', telling her that I was buying them second hand from John and using my wages to do so.

I loved (sea) fishing and four or five of us would regularly get the train down to Newhaven and fish from the breakwater to the west side of the estuary. We'd often spend the night there, too – not sleeping, just fishing. In those days there were plenty of fish in the sea and we would chuck back what are commonly seen on fish counters today (whiting, dogfish (aka rock salmon), gurnard etc) and I would often go home with good sized cod, bass, skate, sole and an abundance of mackerel. One time we caught so much mackerel that we lashed about eight fishing rods together and covered them in plastic to make a mackerel stretcher. That was an interesting train journey home and, at one point, we stopped right over the river outside of Lewes. There was a chap below fishing and we shouted down (train windows opened in those days), asking if he'd caught anything. He shouted back that he hadn't and then around 50-60 mackerel rained down on him before the train began moving!

My biggest catch was from a boat (which I could afford now and again, courtesy of Mrs Bostock) – a 17lb conger eel. It was longer than I was tall. I have no idea how I got it home but I did and my Mum asked what she was supposed to do with it. I suggested she fed it to the cat. She cut off about 10%, which filled the fridge and kept the cat fed for about four weeks, and I put the rest of it in the garage (we didn't own a car). It was about 10 days later that I remembered it and, when I opened the door I was immediately struck by the smell (even worse than Mrs Bostock's house maybe) plus a small mountain of maggots that covered what was left of the eel. Those came in useful for all the boys at school that fished rivers and lakes, increasing my popularity considerably.

I snagged my first proper girlfriend, Sally Gardener from Balcombe, when I was about 14. I say proper in so much as I would go round to her house for tea and she would even sometimes come to ours. Her next door neighbour was Janet Malins and her boyfriend was Mick Tingley, and we became quite close friends. Sally and Janet, along with Jackie Rye from Handcross – who was extremely well-developed for a 14-year-old girl – were the pick of the bunch in our year and so I got the appropriate respect for that. I might have kissed Sally once or twice and I thought I was going to marry her. We must have gone out with each other for over a year but I don't recall how it ended or who went out with her next.

I took my GCE's and did well and was due to go off to sixth form college but, such was my lack of enthusiasm for education, I looked for other ways to fulfil my ambitions and declined the opportunity. This was another decision that my Mum didn't make any attempt to influence.

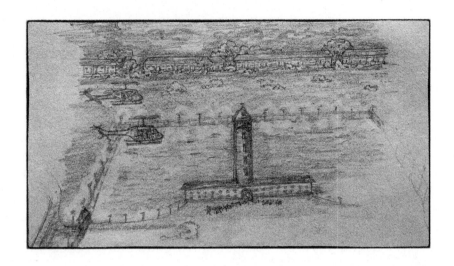

4 - THE WAR YEARS

At 16/17 I was totally rudderless. I had nowhere to really turn and I was making decisions without any real guidance, just relying on instinct. However, my dream was still to be a pilot, and very specifically an Army helicopter pilot. Having turned my back on sixth form college I was in a bit of a jam, but fortunately discovered another route to fulfil my dream. I was able to join the Army as a 'boy soldier' at The Apprentices College in Arborfield, near Reading. The deal was that I would continue my academic education, but also train in mechanical engineering. At the end of the two-year programme, I would walk out with my three A levels, which I studied for in my own time, and then I would go straight to flying school. Well, that was the plan ...

During my two years of academic/technical training, I discovered that learning about anything mechanical was, as easy to me as learning a rare dialect of the Chinese language. To say I was clueless was an understatement but, somehow, I managed to progress through the various checkpoints. Even more problematic was that I didn't like it. In fact, I hated it. But quitting was not an option – I'd signed up for the two years of education (plus three years of service) and that's what I had to do. I think there was an option to 'buy myself out' (of the contract) but I didn't have the money, nor did my Mum, so I was stuck. Worse was yet to come when I was slowly introduced into the flying side of things, I discovered I was terrified of flying! Now, for a kid who had planned on being a pilot for most of his adolescent life, this was a major problem. What on earth do I do? Over the next 18 months I completed my A levels, so at least I had the option of going to University when released from the Army, but I would be 22 by then and that didn't feel right. Thankfully, it was a decision I could defer until later. In the meantime, I became a very poor helicopter engineer and found myself gravitating towards road-going vehicles. I concluded that my lack of skill would be less of a problem if a Land Rover, armoured car or tank broke down rather than a Sioux helicopter at 4,000ft.

During my time at at Arborfield, the one real highlight was learning to play squash. I quickly progressed into the college team and became the established number two player. The number one was a huge black guy who would totally dominate the T (the middle of the court you need to get to in order to play a return shot). He was so huge he occupied it like a rock – and the distance around him was like a small roundabout. Therefore, even though he weighed in at about 17 stone and wasn't particularly mobile, he didn't need to be, because returning any sort of shot was nigh on impossible. I eventually worked him out and became number one and went on to represent the Army youth team. Had they had professional squash players in those days, who knows what might have been, but it became my best sport by a stretch. Unfortunately and almost as soon as I became really proficient my left ankle gave up on me and I neglected to do the proper physio. By the time I was in my mid twenties I simply didn't have the strength in my ankle to continue, at any serious level and I descended the leagues to little better than novice level, it was cruel.

Once I had finished college I was 'posted' to my first regiment in Detmold a small city in North Rhine-Westphalia, Germany. I was attached to one of two regiments of the Household Calvary, namely The Lifeguards. They only had horses for ceremonial occasions, this was a tank regiment, with four squadrons each of six battle tanks – huge beasts weighing in at over 50 tons. I was attached, meaning I was to provide mechanical and technical support, to the 24 tanks. Little did they know how little I knew, well at the outset anyway. I soon discovered that the life of a soldier (of any rank or discipline) was excruciatingly boring and a typical day would involve eating, drinking, listening to music and watching TV, then rinse and repeat.

In our section there was James 'Jazz' Robertson a small but tough, I'm going to say Glaswegian, which probably means he was from Edinburgh. I looked up to him because he drove our tracked armoured vehicle (a 434 for any aficionado's) and I was envious as it was about the only interesting thing to do. Our boss was a giant sized Yorkshireman Les 'Brutus' Benson, I looked up to him because he was about 6'7" tall and built like a rhino. Lastly the unit boss was Warrant Officer Alexander Irwin (Archie) Archibald another Scotsman and I looked up to him because he had a really nice metallic green Ford Capri. The first words he uttered to me were: "If it moves salute it, if it doesn't polish it." Oh, everyone in the forces has a nickname but I genuinely don't recall mine, I doubt it would have been flattering.

Detmold was a miserable place, think the Medway towns and carry on downhill. The local population were pretty anti and who can blame them? They didn't want 500/600 British Army personnel polluting their town and so I rarely ventured out. On the few occasions I did it was pretty unpleasant. Only a handful of bars welcomed the British and because of that they were packed to the rafters with squaddies dressed in their cheap suits and stinking of even cheaper after shave. No locals would go near these places apart from half a dozen or so girls who 'did the rounds' and who often were the cause of quite violent fights and so most of downtown Detmold was swarming with Military Police on a Friday/Saturday. I really didn't see the point of going out. My pay was so miserable I couldn't afford a car and so I was trapped within the immediate vicinity. The highlight of any night out was the currywurst van parked outside the entrance to the barracks. Indeed after a very short time it was the only place I would ever really go.

Such was the state of armed forces financing back then, we weren't allowed to practice anything like war games more than once or twice a year. The reason why we had so many troops in Germany was to counter the threat from any potential Russian aggression – we were there, on the so called front line, ready and prepared to respond to the Soviet threat. Every day we would make sure everything was in place for an imminent attack. The soldiers would be cleaning their tanks, painting them with yet more camouflage, polishing rifles, ironing trousers and generally being at a state of high alert. Our technical teams would be making sure that their main fighting equipment was properly maintained and ready to go. The reality wasn't really that, it was more tokenism, a gesture I think.

My first major exercise (war game) was a 10-day simulated battle on Lunerberg Heath about 20 miles to the north. We were teaming up with two regiments of infantry and a light armour regiment and were taking on (fighting) a joint German/Belgium force. At 06.30 on an absolutely freezing February morning the 24 tanks rolled out of the barracks for the short journey north. 'Crowds' of Army wives and children had gathered outside to witness the spectacle, some even waved flags for goodness sake. There was even the odd curious local or two that didn't hate the fact that their town/country was occupied by perma pissed squaddies, or perhaps they did? The tank commanders sat proud atop their turrets as they left the barracks waving as they went as if they would never be seen again. The whole scene was absurd in the extreme, it's only a frigging game! The journey was due to take about an hour. Some of the tanks made it to the destination, actually about seven or eight of the 24, the rest had broken down at various points en route. We were sent out to fix and/or recover the casualties. I think it took another four days to get all the equipment to the destination. I could only assume that in a real combat situation the Ruskies probably wouldn't have waited around for us to get our act together. This situation was repeated every time, a sad reflection on our military capabilities.

I put up with this for nearly a year but I had to get away for the sake of my sanity and so I did the only thing possible and that was to volunteer for active service in Northern Ireland. It was a radical thing to do but the only other option was desertion which seemed even less sensible. So with that I soon found myself in Armagh, a border town that was firmly at the very sharp end of what was as close to a war as I was ever to experience. Our base was a converted bus station and there were about 200 of us jammed into an area the size of a Sainsburys Local. The only soldiers who were allowed out were those who did their four hours off and four hours on patrol in converted commercial vehicles. The army called them 'Armoured Cars' but the armour was poor and totally ineffective in stopping even a cheap Chinese armour-piercing bullet. My first experience of knowing people that had died was very difficult to absorb particularly when the deaths were not only senseless, but could have been avoided. I was attached to an infantry regiment (The Royal Green Jackets) looking after their equipment but it didn't require too much effort, and I quickly became as bored in Northern Ireland as I was in Germany. Given the soldiers were patrolling so much (up to 16 hours a day) and only given three days off in four months, I would occasionally volunteer to go on a foot patrol in the city and allow someone else a little rest. Those 'walks' were real eye-openers. For the most part we were so very unwelcome and were sworn at, spat at and universally derided. It was an altogether very unpleasant and sometimes scary experience. But it did have it's lighter moments too. One time I volunteered to do a patrol into town and the commander decided to go into a pub and carry out a face and ID check on the customers in there (no wonder we were popular). One group we checked were off duty police officers, they were chatty and they ended up buying us beers. We didn't realise that a special branch officer was sat in the corner observing all of this, we were reported and that led to another dressing down and extra duties of some sort. I didn't volunteer for patrol again.

I was in Northern Ireland at the height of the troubles in 1974/75. Back home, the red top tabloids were whipping up loads of support from their readers: 'Give our boys in Ireland some support"; "Donate and we can get them some TVs", etc. Such was the success of these campaigns that I think millions of pounds were raised, which meant we almost all had our own TV! With no headphones it could be quite difficult to watch your own 26" TV in a small room with 10 other TV's going.

One day my boss called me and said that our technical team had been give a sackful of money and he had decided to buy two speedboats and put them on Lough Erne. As a result, he wanted me to transfer to Omagh and be responsible for their upkeep. The idea was that when the troops got their few days off in the middle of a four-month tour, they could relax and recuperate and I could take them on boat rides and teach water skiing, alongside my regular job of course. I duly accepted my new assignment, got the hell out of Armagh and was subsequently attached to another cavalry regiment, the 9th/12th Royal Lancers as the official speedboat driver.

Everything went well in Omagh and I became a very accomplished water skier. As the regiment I was now attached to was on a long-term tour (18 months) there were some special privileges. First and foremost, we were allowed out, but this benefit was subject to very strict rules relating to where we could and couldn't go and the times that we were allowed out. For the most part, we ignored the 'where' bit, and it did get a bit hairy at times. We were also allowed a disco in our camp, which meant that every other Saturday coachloads of young ladies would be brought in, security checked and let loose in what was the main bar area. It was a free-for-all! One Saturday my mate Dick Pienear, a very dodgy fella from Romford (more on him later) got talking to two girls and we spent the evening with them. They had a strict leaving time of 11.00pm and, before leaving, the girls suggested we get out and meet them on the outside. Even though we weren't allowed out at that time of night, Dick and I, now well under the influence of alcohol, thought we would give it a try. As you might guess, Army bases in Northern Ireland were very well protected and made to be impregnable, but we had an idea! We got ourselves down to the furthest perimeter away from anything and we decided we could scale the 20ft fence and get out. We started climbing the wire fence and about half way up we heard the sound of what I imagined to be a very big and very hungry dog, followed by the words: "Halt! Who goes there?". I think we both hoped he actually hadn't seen us – just heard a noise – so we carried on climbing. No more than three feet from the top we are blasted with a high-power torch and more warnings, which I think included the word "shoot". But we were so near to 'freedom' so I kept clambering, caught the barbed wire at the top and managed to scramble over in what would have been a near world record time if this were a sport. Dick, however, froze on the spot and then slowly retreated back down. I think his actions might have distracted the guard, so I got myself down to the bottom and headed off across fields at rocket like speed and into the unknown.

Miraculously, I managed to find my way to the spot where the girls had told us to go and even more surprising was that they were both there. They were disappointed that I was alone and even more disappointed that I was not in party mood as during my sprint across the fields it struck me that the bigger problem for me would actually be getting back in without being spotted (military bases are set up to stop people getting in, not out). Plus Dick would have been interrogated into revealing who his accomplice was. I was in deep poo.

I stayed with the girls for about two hours, had a coffee or two to sober up and made my way back to the camp under the cover of darkness. It might have been OK for Daniel Craig but not me, I should have just walked up and surrendered. I found a good-looking spot far away from the main gates and started to scale the fence. I got about 5ft up before I was apprehended. I was thrown in the guard house jail and the next morning I was up in front of Regimental Adjutant for a real dressing down. Bottom line, I was put on seven days guard duty: four hours on and four hours off for the entire time.

I had never done guard duty, I had an idea what its

purpose was but that was about it. The four hours on was up a ladder into a covered wooden box about 6ft square, while the four hours off was a bunk bed at the bottom of the ladder. Meals were brought in during the down time and were of a standard I would expect in a run-down South American prison. I reported at 08.00 to be told to go up into the box and I can come down at 12.00. "Keep your eyes peeled," they would order me. Given my work in the Army, I had hardly ever fired a gun and the nearest I got to guard experience was by watching The Great Escape at least half a dozen times as well as almost every episode of Hogans Heroes! The box contained a phone (no dial on it so I couldn't call home), a torch (I was told not to switch it on as a sniper would see me, which made me wonder what it was there for), a pair of binoculars and a huge machine gun on a tripod. A big belt of ammunition ran through the gun, with each fifth bullet having a phosphorous tip, which lit up in travel, making it easy to aim at night. The only other thing in the box was a small metal tube (around two inches long) poking out of the wall below the gun.

I really wanted to shoot that machine gun. My view was a main road about 30m ahead of me and a row of semi detached houses, which fronted a large estate. Boring would have been a massive exaggeration. I would train my gun on various passers by and also the helicopters that regularly travelled up and down patrolling the border with the South. On the fourth night, dead beat and bored silly, I started examining that little tube and wondered why it was there. To hang something on, perhaps? Maybe it was a base for something that poked in it. I stuck my finger down it and the most god awful siren (sirens, actually) went off that I can imagine would have been heard five miles away. All the floodlights around the perimeter of the base lit up and within two minutes there were about 100 armed troops running to pre designated stations and two helicopters had been scrambled. My phone was ringing but I couldn't answer it because I was in a state of utter shock. Next thing, there was banging on the floor beneath my feet. I lifted the hatch to see the grizzly Guard Commander staring daggers and shrieking at me, asking what the **** was I doing! Things did eventually settle down and I was replaced in the box and put back in the jail. The next morning I was up in front of the Adjutant again and I pleaded my innocence by explaining that I had never performed guard duty in my life and nobody had told me what to do. Unbelievably, not only did I get off without further punishment, the remaining three days of my guard duty was cancelled as I was clearly not guard material!

Within our base at Omagh we had a large Air Corps detachment of around 80 men plus all the engineers so some 150 of us in total . Because we were set aside from the main regiment we were our own, largely self-contained community. That meant we were allowed our own private bar, which was attached to the workshops and aircraft hangers. We also had our own football team that played in the Northern Ireland Army league against teams from other parts of the province. Because we were only 150 men – and most regiments and HQ wings were 400+ – we weren't hugely successful, but it passed time on a Friday or Saturday afternoon. When we played at home it was traditional that we invited the opposition into our bar and they would stay for an hour and have a pint or two. One particularly memorable game was when we played a team from Belfast Headquarters. We were midway through the second half when one of our unused subs (Noggin is all I remember him as) stumbled onto the pitch for no good reason. We shouted at him to get off but he ignored us and staggered around like a drunk man before collapsing. The ref stopped the game and we went to investigate. He looked bad and straight away he was given mouth-to-mouth resuscitation. In an instant, a medic was called and an ambulance arrived to take him away. Oddly, I recall we got 13 minutes of injury time added. Noggin died later that day from a massive heart attack.

We painted all the windows of our private bar black because it was supposed to close at 11.00pm, to be consistent with the main squaddies bar. However, blacking out the windows allowed us to stay all night if we wanted to, as long as we were reasonably quiet. One of the windows was broken, so we replaced it painted it black and then, in white over the top, named it the 'Noggin memorial window' He would have liked that.

One very wet and horrid winter Friday afternoon, we had a home game and, after the final whistle at around 3.30pm, we did our traditional invitation to the bar. The opposing team came in, had a beer or two and departed about 5.00pm. By 8.00pm most had left to have their showers and dinner, but six or seven of us stayed on. We used to play cards a lot, so once that started on that evening, it went on and on ... and on! By Saturday afternoon, we had no real food left except for a huge jar of pickled eggs. But we still had loads of beer, barrels of draught Guinness and Smithwick's. The final four of us eventually left the bar at around 06.30 Monday morning, still in our football kit and boots, headed off to the shower and were ready for work at 08.00. I worked out we were there for 63 hours, on a diet of draught beer, a few pies and sandwiches for the first 24 hours and then, five or six pickled eggs each. It doesn't leave much to the imagination!

Some of the lads had their own cars, which was handy when we were allowed out. Steve Dawson had a really flashy (in those days) Bond Bug. It was a three-wheeler, but a sporty two-seater and fast, due to its body being made entirely of fibreglass. The roof flipped forward to get in and then, when seated, you pulled down on a handle that locked you in. It was Steve's pride and joy – almost brand new and he was always cleaning and polishing it. One day Dodgy Dick from Romford came to my room waving a set of car keys in his hand and a wearing a huge grin. He told me that Steve had to go back home for hospital treatment as he had developed yellow jaundice. Before doing so he had loaned Dick his car so we could use it to go out if we wished. A few days later Dick told me we had permission (from the company admin office) to go to a pub in Tyrone on the Saturday night, it was a busy pub with music and considered safe as it was staunchly protestant. He drove the nine miles to the pub, which was busy – we were really happy to be 'free'. We got some looks when we walked in, but nothing that was too intimidating and it was clear there were other soldiers in there too. Dick got in with a pretty girl and I didn't. It transpired that she lived in Omagh too and Dick offered her a lift home. My immediate thoughts being that three didn't go into two (the car).

He told me I should drive and somehow he would be able to sit the girl on his lap in the passenger seat. I wasn't convinced but he refused to entertain the thought that she would sit on my lap. I got in and Dick climbed into the passenger seat before the girl hoisted herself in onto his lap. It was very, very cramped indeed – she had to angle herself across my seat to allow the roof down but even then it kept bouncing off her head and I couldn't get it to catch. Eventually when she almost had her head in my groin I managed to get it shut. It was a foggy night and what with her spread halfway across me and the lights not being the brightest, driving conditions were difficult. About two miles outside Omagh, the road was quite highly elevated, with no barriers either side and a 40ft straight drop into a boggy field on either side. Even now I don't know what happened – I may have hit something in the road with the single front wheel, or maybe I just steered straight off. But, the next thing I remember is having no road whatsoever underneath us and the car flying through the air in a scene reminiscent of something out of Back to the Future. We landed with a thud and the next thing was the most curious of sounds, a bit like a large egg breaking. If I passed out it was only for seconds, but when I came to I was sat in the drivers seat, hands firmly grasping the steering wheel but the entire body of the car was gone. Not only was it gone but it was strewn across the field in what looked like thousands of little pieces. Dick was about 20ft ahead of me, getting to his feet and the girl was another 10ft further on, legs akimbo and groaning. I got my seat belt off, struggled over and, while she had quite a nasty cut to her head, I concluded that she wasn't in any serious trouble. What seemed like seconds later, an ambulance and a police car show up and we are all taken away to the general hospital and given a thorough examination. Thankfully we are all OK and were discharged with a few minor cuts and bruises. I was breathalysed and it came up negative, but it was close.

There was nothing left of the car. It was quite possibly swept up and put in a bin bag. We now had the issue of telling Steve, who was due back from hospital in the next couple of weeks. That wasn't going to be fun, or easy. Together, Dick and I went through various scenarios – none of which included the third passenger – before settling on a puncture. We learned the date that Steve was returning and prepared our story. That morning I went round to Dick's room to get our final story totally aligned. Dick wasn't there but his room-mate told me he had returned to London the previous night for some spurious reason like his Mum was ill. Ha! He'd had left me to face the music alone. Steve came around to my room once he got back, obviously and understandably furious. He stopped short of giving me a good hiding, even though he quite easily could have done. He screamed and bawled at me, giving me no chance whatsoever to offer him our story. Indeed, it quickly became clear that no explanation would suffice as one of the main reasons for his upset was that he never told Dick he could use his car. He merely gave him the keys and asked him to turn the engine over now and again to keep the battery charged.

Dick eventually returned but I don't recall how that played out with Steve. What I do know is that I paid Steve back every penny for his car. It was a real challenge, but I did it and was glad that I did.

A few months later I left the Army after four eventful, but unfulfilled, years and without any kind of plan or idea of what I was going to do next. I had actually been awarded a medal for my work in Ireland which I was able to wear with pride at Remembrance Day parades. It wouldn't have been inappropriate had it been awarded for services in the face of extreme boredom. I still have it somewhere and occasionally see it and reflect on those times.

Back in 1976 all I knew was that I didn't want to go home to my Mum in Haywards Heath and that I needed a job pronto. Paying back Steve for his car had completely wiped out my savings, plus I still had a monthly commitment to him which I was determined to settle. I had to do something and do it pretty quickly.

5 - BRIGHTON AND HOVE,
THE START OF TRANSIENCE

I don't think I stayed at my Mum's for more than two weeks before I had replied to an ad in Brighton's local newspaper – the Evening Argus – and moved into a flat-share on Compton Road with a fella by the name of Gerry. He was about 10 years older than me and had, until recently, been the landlord of a pub on Western Road. He had lost his driving licence after being caught drink-driving and, with it, his job. Gerry had moved in to the flat a few weeks before me. He was a decent type, fairly quiet and gave me my space.

I somehow managed to blag a job at a Fiat/Lancia main dealership in Burgess Hill, about 10 miles north of Brighton, as a mechanic. I think they were impressed by my military technical training, even though my ability to actually put any of it into practice was very limited, well nil to be precise. I bought some cheap tools and did what I thought was the most mundane work: changing oil and filters; tightening wheels, etc. It was a total bore. I studied the other fellas there. Don had been doing the job 30 years and every Friday afternoon the Snap On tools man would come around in his van after we had been paid (cash in brown envelope). Don and the others were like kids in a candy shop and would spend a sizeable proportion of their not very large wage on a new spanner, socket set or some other tool. Not me, I would beg or borrow most of my tools from others, which didn't make me popular. I hated the job and hated that I stank of diesel or grease 24/7, no matter how hard I tried to clean myself up. After a few weeks I decide being the Snap-On tool man was the way to go, he was raking it in and had his own transport too. Unfortunately I discover it's a franchise with a hefty franchise fee, and it was obvious why that was the case.

I recall one Saturday night ending up in the Top Rank nightclub and bagging a slow dance with a girl in a pale yellow blouse. It was routinely hot and sweaty in there and after our dance she turned away to return to her seat and I was aghast to see two very clear and dark hand prints on her back. I went into work on the Monday and quit.

I was forced to 'sign on' for unemployment benefit (£9 a week back then) and scoured the Evening Argus for jobs. One, in particular, stood out. Partly because it was it appeared every night and also because it offered unlimited riches after a brief period of training. Gerry decided he would apply too, because he wasn't doing much other than casual work in a variety of bars in town. It was a job selling insurance. I remember the interview well. It was with a very polished South African who asked me my name, address, what I had done before and why I wanted the job. I obviously did well as he offered it to me there and then and suggested I attend my first training session that afternoon. I caught up with Gerry and coincidentally he had the same offer, as indeed had everyone else that showed up for an interview that morning! We went off for lunch and came back and discovered there were about 15 people on our training course. Training lasted about three hours and basically comprised learning a short script, which would be delivered on the doorsteps of potential customers. It went: "Good evening, my name is Tony Cooper, from Liberty Life and I wonder if I could interest you in paying less tax." That opener then led to a pitch to have them sign up to a monthly, life insurance-backed savings plan that would mature in 25 or 30 years' time and pay absurdly huge returns. This was 1976 and the industry hadn't even thought about regulation.

My first night was that night, there was little point doing this during the day as we needed working people. I was put into a car with my team leader and two others and driven to Hollingbury, a not great estate on the East side of Brighton, where we began knocking on doors. I didn't do or say anything much except observe my team leader and, in the three hours we were out, we had the door slammed in our faces more than a dozen times. Not only that, we were threatened a few times too. However, the team leader also made a few sales and he told me that his three hours had made him about the equivalent of £500. That money would be paid at the end of the week once the first cheque for the premium had cleared and then he would get another £500 in 12 months time if the policy was still active. £500 back then was ...... lots.

Our working day was from about 2.00pm to 10.00pm, sometimes later depending on where we went. The first hour was a 'Ra Ra' with the South African who got us all fired up and then we would be off in the car to some low grade estate to peddle our wares. I was extremely successful to start with. I don't recall exactly how much I was making, but it was enough to pay Steve Dawson back and allow me to miss the odd day because, money apart, I didn't enjoy the work at all. The hours were antisocial, the amount of abuse I got was horrid and I knew, deep down, that the product was a rip-off although I wasn't entirely sure I knew why. On top of that, I was then introduced to 'clawback'. This was a mechanism where my commission for selling policies that week was reduced because policies I'd sold in previous weeks were to buyers who had a change of heart and stopped their payments so the policies lapsed. We hadn't been warned of that!

One of the team leaders, Simon, a scrawny ex-public

schoolboy was a real 'ducker and diver', but very convincing and one of the top earners. It was 1976 and there was a huge potato shortage. He came to Gerry and me one day saying he had access to 10,000 tonnes of high-grade Kenyan Whites, which were on a ship in the channel. If we could sell them at what seemed like a reasonable price we would would make a killing and he would split the money three ways. There was between £3-4,000 each for us. We got nowhere with the obvious targets (supermarkets), but I had the idea to approach a crisp producer and managed to make contact with a buyer of Smith's Crisps, one of the largest at the time. He was completely sold and we did the (informal) deal very easily. Then it was just a question of getting delivery and all the paperwork agreed, which Simon said he had in hand. Unfortunately, the potatoes never showed up. The story given was that we had been usurped by an Irish business and the ship had landed the spuds at some remote port in South East Ireland. I was not convinced. Simon promised to make it up to us, saying he had a number of "irons in the fire" and would definitely give us another opportunity.

A couple of weeks later, he approached us and told us he had access to 10,000 bottles of premium scotch whiskey that he could get for £1 a bottle (it retailed at £6). Same deal: if we could shift it then he would split the profits three ways. I assumed it was stolen, but I didn't ask so I didn't know.

Gerry reckoned he knew people that would buy the

Scotch and one day he announced that he had set up a 'meet' with Syd Minter (Dad of Alan Minter, the British and European Boxing Middleweight boxing champion). Syd had a bit of a reputation – gangster might have been a bit of a stretch, but he was definitely someone that I suspect knew a trick or two. He had a private drinking club in a square off the seafront in Hove and we went down there one late afternoon and rapped on the door. A small hatch opened and we were peering at a pair of eyes.

"Yeah?"

"Oh hi, is Syd there?"

"Who wants him?"

"Gerry."

"Hang on."

The hatch shuts and a minute later the door opens and we are standing in front of a short 50-something man with greased back grey hair, flanked by two giants in ill-fitting cheap suits. Gerry launched into his sales pitch and Syd didn't seem to be paying much attention, but when Gerry had finished Syd said he would have the lot for £3 a bottle. A quick calculation and that was £20,000 profit for us, needless to say though I wasn't convinced. Syd then wrapped up by saying (in the most intimidating South London accent) "this had better be straight up Gerry, my old son. I don't like being dicked around, you know what I mean?". He then told us we could go to the bar and have whatever we wanted and it was all on the house. I was as nervous as hell and very quickly I was prepared to give up my share of the £20,000 as the experience of the Kenyan Whites was now haunting me. As you might imagine, the Scotch never showed up and I was now convinced that it was just a figment of imagination in Simon's mind. I don't know how Gerry got out of it but, give him his due, he went back to see Syd and managed to escape without any serious injury.

My insurance selling career ended a few weeks after the potato/whiskey incidents whilst door knocking on a dreadful council estate in Streatham. I was on the third floor of a run-down apartment block, where the front doors opened to an outside walkway with a waist-high wall to the other side. I knocked on one door and a huge man answered. When I introduced myself and my tax-saving initiative he took a huge swing at me, knocking me back into the wall with such force that I very nearly went over the edge to what would have been certain death. I never knocked on another door again.

So I was now unemployed again and, with no idea what I wanted to do. I once again scoured the Evening Argus and was taken by an advertisement for a new American Bank (money shop) that was going to be opening a branch in Brighton and wanted a management trainee. It paid a salary (£208 a month) and looked respectable. Interviews were being held all day at the Job Centre the following week and I managed to get a slot. I was interviewed by a young personnel (HR) manager who I could tell liked me and, the next day, I got a call from her saying I had been successful and that I was to go to the company's head office in Bracknell for a final interview with her boss, the Personnel Director, a couple of days later.

The company was called HFC Trust & Savings – huge in the US but the Brighton branch would be only its ninth since first opening in the UK seven months earlier, so it was still very small. When I arrived for my interview in Bracknell I was told that the Personnel Director was off sick, so I was to meet with the Managing Director. Jim MacDonald was a 50-something American from Chicago and one of the most impressive people I had ever met (possibly because I hadn't met that many impressive people) and a giant of a man in every respect. He obviously hadn't looked at my (four-page) application before I arrived and did so after I was introduced. We sat in silence for five minutes as he went through it. When he had finished he looked up offered some weak apology and told me that he didn't think I had the right background and experience, plus they wanted graduates. He was sorry that I had been dragged up to see him and asked me how much it had cost me to get there, before buzzing his PA and asking her to bring cash to reimburse me. While waiting for her, he made small talk and I knew that this was my only opportunity so I worked really hard to try and turn his thinking to something more positive. It was several minutes before his PA brought in an envelope with my cash and he put it to one side and allowed me to continue the conversation. In doing so, it turned into more of an interview-style discussion and, less than an hour later, he offered me the job! I was delighted. It really was my first bona-fide job and something that offered real prospects as they had a hugely ambitious expansion plan. From that day on, Jim took a very close interest in my progress – no favouritism at all, he wasn't like that - and he become my mentor and I regarded him as something of a father figure.

My boss, the Brighton branch manager, was Sam Cohen. He was on a two-year assignment from the US and he came from Johnstown, Pennsylvania – a place he described as even less desirable than Creepy Crawley. Sam was young, very committed and took my training very seriously. He delivered my learning via a set of training manuals and materials that the company had developed over years in the US and that had been badly Anglicised. Although it had positioned itself in the market as a new way of banking – without the formalities of typical banks – HFC was really just a money-lending institution. It did offer bank accounts and savings accounts, but all of its promotional activity was aimed at lending money to those who wanted an easier way to borrow than being subjected to interrogation by their bank manager, which was the norm for most people in those days. As someone once said, a bank was a place where you could borrow money only if you could prove you didn't need to. I took my new career seriously and did very well.

During this time one of my friends, Andy Sullivan, was a teacher at one of the many language schools in Brighton. These language schools attracted 'well-to-do' young men and women from affluent families all over the world and courses would run from three to twelve months. The fees were eye-wateringly high and it always puzzled me that most of these students were very proficient in English when they arrived (I went to several welcoming parties) and not obviously more proficient when they left (I also went to several farewell parties). At one welcoming party I met Rosita, a well-heeled Swiss girl from Berne. She would be 'studying' and experiencing our culture for six months. We hit it off and soon became boyfriend and girlfriend. Her life was very easy going because she would study for four hours a day and the rest of the time was spent socialising and travelling around and exploring the South of England. I suppose she was my first proper girlfriend. She had driven her car - an orange Mini with Swiss number plates and (obviously) left-hand-drive - over from Switzerland when she started her course. One night we decided to go into Brighton for a meal and she drove. We went to one of the many Italian pizza places and shared a bottle of wine. After dinner, she wasn't feeling too good and I volunteered to drive, which might not have been a great idea as I suspect I had drunk the majority of the wine. But we were in central Brighton and it wasn't too far. We set off up West Street and as we were passing Churchill Square I noticed blue flashing lights in my mirror. "Damn!" I said and pulled over. The policeman came to the 'driver's' window which Rosita rolled down, because it was actually the passenger window in a left-hooker. Anyway, he looked through at me and said: "Do you realise, sir, that you are driving without lights?" Before I had any opportunity to reply, Rosita interjected with "I'm sorry officer, my friend doesn't speak English." That threw him a little, but it threw me a whole lot more and the ensuing conversation was comical in the extreme:

Policeman (to Rosita): Can you ask him for his driving licence, please?

Rosita (turning to me): Hast du deinen führerschein?

Me (while patting my pockets): Ich nich dich stich negst unda svetten.

Rosita (turning to policeman): I'm sorry officer, he doesn't have it with him.

Policeman: Does he have any ID with him?

Rosita (to me): Haben Sie einen Ausweis?

Me: Ich nicht dikov donner und blitzen sturm-bannfuhrer.

Rosita (to policeman): No he hasn't. He has been moving house and it is all packed in a box somewhere.

At this point I was quite sure I was going to be asked to leave the car and be arrested or breathalysed, but he persevered with another couple of questions to which he received increasingly ridiculous answers and then admitted defeat. He told Rosita to tell me to be more careful in the future and went back to his Panda car.

My relationship with Rosita blossomed but, after six months, she finished her course and returned to Switzerland. I tried to continue the relationship from afar but we were too young to make that work and we inevitability drifted apart.

Meanwhile, at work, after eight months as a trainee branch manager I finished my training and was promoted to assistant manager. There was only a token pay rise, but more important, it was a significant step forward on my fledgling career path.

The company was expanding quickly and was opening a branch every three or four weeks. I was told I was being given an opportunity to take on a new assignment as assistant manager at one of Derby, Lewisham or Chatham. Derby had just knocked Brighton out of the FA Cup, so that one was definitely out. Lewisham had been all but raised to the ground following a period of civil unrest, so Chatham was an easy choice. I quit my flat, packed my one or two bags, got the train up to Kent and checked into a cheap B&B, which the company agreed to pay for two weeks. Looking back, that move was step one in what was going to be a very transient life – the house we live in now is the thirteenth home I have owned. I'm not sure if that's good or bad, but I've certainly 'seen the world'!

6 - GROWING UP, WELL SORT OF

Life in Chatham – one of the three joined-together Medway towns – was fairly uneventful. In fact, my life as a whole had become pretty dull and boring, which was a good reflection of the place I had found myself in. I didn't realise what a vibrant and alive town Brighton was until I went to the Medway towns. I couldn't see anything to commend the place for at all. It was grey, had a distinctly unpleasant smell about it and the people weren't particularly welcoming.

After two weeks in my B&B I had made no progress on renting anywhere, partly because there was little available but also due to my obscenely low salary, which priced me out of all but doss houses. I was *forced* to move in with my sister (who lived close to my office), her husband and their two young children - as well as an array of family pets. I love and care for my sister, but she fitted the stereotype of a Medway town resident pretty well - her life was fairly mundane and they never really did very much or went anywhere. But she was a good mother and a very caring sister. I never was able to get used to the fact that her dinner choice would be determined by the day of the week, so every Monday would be spaghetti bolognese, cottage pie on a Wednesday, Friday fish and chips, etc. I hated prawn salad, so I made a point of working late on Tuesdays! She also had an uncanny knack of cooking food that I could only describe as soggy, she could even manage to stew an egg.

I made frantic efforts to find a place to rent for myself. In desperation I saw an ad in the local paper asking for a fourth girl to share a house with three others. I asked our receptionist at work to call, explain my predicament and try to convince them that I was an honourable and decent chap and they should at least meet me. Surprisingly they did and their 'leader', Ruth, was kind enough to give me a chance, which meant Fish Fridays were no more. The three girls were all British Caledonian cabin crew and worked on the South American routes, which was great for me for two reasons. Firstly, in those days a South American trip would last for 10 or more as it involved internal flights between Buenos Aires and Lima, which meant I often had the house to myself and could do as I wished. I'm not talking about anything more exciting than leave my rubbish strewn around with no consequences. Secondly, when the girls returned they would be loaded with food and booze that they had taken from the aircraft. This was a godsend to me as I was so broke, paying well over half of my take home pay on rent, that those days were amongst the few that I actually ate properly. I lived a feast and famine life. This situation, coupled with the fact that the Medway towns were such a dump, allowed me to focus on my job to the exclusion of pretty well anything else. Eight months later I had completed all my training and a few weeks after that, I received THE call! I was being promoted to branch manager of a brand new site opening in Kingswood, Bristol. I was to be there the following Monday where I would meet my new boss, Colin Pryor.

Kingswood was a nice district on the east side of Bristol and my big, new, shiny branch office was in a newly developed shopping precinct. My staff were a receptionist and a management trainee, Gerry. I was given 4 weeks accommodation in a hotel and so I quickly set about finding a flat to rent. Getting promoted meant a pay rise, but it was derisory and I think the reason might have been that I was also given a company car and the company hierarchy thought that might have been reward enough. I was still totally broke, but at least I had a brand new, puke brown, Ford Escort (RDP 67R) to sit in! I found a nice little one-bed flat in Fishponds, a quiet area towards the city centre, moved in and settled down.

I enjoyed a lot about Bristol, it was young (two

universities) and had lots going on. I suppose after the Medway towns even a remote village in Northumberland might be exciting but I thoroughly enjoyed my time there … mostly. The people took a bit of getting used to and the local greeting of "Arr right moy luuuuv" became very tedious. The other thing that struck me was that everyone knew everyone else, so the feeling of being an outsider was very strong and tough to deal with. In those days, we had paper phone books and, because Bristol was a large city, so was the phone book. It was very striking that even the most unusual of names could run to several pages and the more common would run to scores, in some respects it was pretty scary!

The business went mad, there were times when we had people queuing out of the doors, I even asked myself if we were doing something wrong. But we weren't and it was simply a reflection of the inability of the traditional banks to connect with their core customers. We were regularly at, or near, the top of the best performing branches (up to 30 at this point) of the month. It was during this time that I recognised that success was not so much about one's own ability and drive, but perhaps more about those who worked for you - and Gerry (and others that soon joined) was very good. As a philosophy, recognising and tapping into the capabilities of others - and motivating them to deliver results - became the cornerstone of my later success and I put it down to those early days in Bristol. We grew the business so rapidly that over the next nine months I had promoted Gerry to assistant manager and recruited a further three management trainees. My success hadn't gone unnoticed and, within the year, I was promoted to a larger, more established branch in Preston.

Preston is in Lancashire – quite simply point the car north and keep going and going and going. Before going there for the first time, my travels in England had never taken me north of London and I was so surprised by the distance, I thought we lived in a small country. I knew that my social life, much of which was still centred around Brighton, would need to change. The branch was an older established one and had come into the business after the acquisition of Niagara Finance the previous year. Unsurprisingly, Niagara was a Canadian finance company and some of its business practices were questionable, to say the least. The outgoing manager (Bryan McBain) had somehow managed to get himself promoted to a larger branch. I say somehow, because this business was all about lending and it seemed that almost every loan was in some stage of default. I had been sent there to sort that out, but I had no experience of how that could be done. I had six staff: two assistant managers; two trainees and two cashier/receptionists. They were generally OK, but demotivated and so I worked on that aspect, mostly in the great pubs that adorn Preston. A lot of time was spent visiting customers in default at their homes, this really was trench warfare and a very tough period and more than once I considered giving up. To show willing, I would often accompany my assistants when they went to meet people. Goodness me, I had never seen or even imagined this level of deprivation. I can't even begin to describe it but, for example, one customer we visited had no furniture in their house other than a couch and a TV (we had financed both, I think). They had three young children and I wonder if they even had beds to sleep in. The front door of the house (on a dreadful council estate) had the words 'Det colecktors **** off we aint got any money' daubed on it in red paint. So much of the business in the office was like this but it was sometimes difficult to sympathise with people that, while being on limited income, prioritised such things as the TV, cigarettes and booze before paying their rent or utility bills – or even, perhaps, putting decent food on the table (or floor in some cases) for their children. It was really heartbreaking to see such self inflicted poverty.

After six months of renting and now on a reasonable salary, I purchased my first house. It was in the village of Much Hoole about eight miles from Preston on the road to Liverpool. It was a relatively new semi, which cost the princely sum of £19,250. I remember feeling very proud of myself, to have achieved this at the ripe old age of 25.

My social life was fairly limited. I mixed a little with the other guys in the branch, but I knew my stay in Preston was going to be fairly temporary and so I focussed a lot on my work. Over the course of the next year we wrote a huge amount of money off to bad debt but, thankfully, we also improved the quality of our business quite dramatically and so slowly the mixture of good to bad improved. Such was the turnaround that I received another promotion, to what was the largest branch (of which there were now 70) in the country. That branch was also in Bristol, right in the city centre, I was thrilled to be getting such an assignment and happy to be going back to Bristol.

I was now 26 and the branch had over 3,000 customers and 10 staff. It was also a training branch where assistant managers from other branches would come for their final assessment. That meant they effectively ran my branch for two weeks – under my supervision – and I had the final say as to whether they should be promoted or not! This was heaven, I had so very little to do and I very quickly totally mastered the art of delegation!

With the benefit of my previous experience of Bristol I made the smart move of buying a house on a brand new small development (15 houses) to the north of the city centre, near the Parkway railway station. It was a fairly typical four-bed detached but, being a new build, I assumed that my 14 neighbours would all be unknown to each other and integration would be easier. Wrong! I'm not sure how, but it was as if everyone knew everyone else as soon as they moved in and I was most certainly the only non-Bristolian on the development. That said, most of my neighbours were friendly and very much the typical 30-somethings with 2.2 children, so I was a bit of a novelty to most of them. The lady in the show house, Kate, was nice and I would often spend my 'down time' in there. We eventually started seeing each other.

There were now four branches in Bristol and the nearest to mine was only a short walk away in Penn Street. All four of us branch managers got along well, so much so that we would meet up regularly for a drink and a game of snooker after work (well, it was technically *during* work, but we deserved some time off) once a week. The nearest branch to me was no more than a 5/6 minute walk and, after a short time a new manager, Andy Pickard, was installed there. I knew Andy as he had come to me a few months earlier for his last two weeks of training. It was good to have another out of towner to socialise with.

During the first summer in Bristol I decided I wanted to buy a boat and get back into water-skiing. One of the guys in my office did a bit of it and told me how he and friends launched their boat under the Severn bridge at Chepstow and then skied up and down the river Wye, the estuary of which comes out by the bridge. At that time, Bristol docks was also the venue for the British leg of the Formula 1 powerboat Grand Prix and the thrill of seeing boats travelling at over 100mph in such a small area certainly whetted my appetite.

I did my research (bear in mind this was pre-internet days) and settled on buying a fairly standard powerboat

(I refused to call it speedboat), designed and built by a former powerboat champion, Doug Driver. I ordered an 18ft boat, which is fairly large for a novice and was asked what size engine I wanted. I asked what they suggested and was told 50-75 horsepower, so I ordered it with a 150 horsepower engine! The boat duly arrived, I had a tow ball fitted to the car and practised driving, reversing and manoeuvring in the street outside my house. For anyone that didn't know me I became 'the bloke with the big boat' and attracted every 6-12-year-old boy to my driveway for several weeks. I finally decided I was good enough to tow the boat on the open road. I had read the instruction manual from cover to cover and I was pretty sure I knew how to get the boat into the water too, so I was all set for my maiden voyage. My mother was coming to stay for a weekend and I thought she was the perfect person to help me out and so we set off to Chepstow on the M4 at what I recall were speeds not exceeding 30mph.

If you've never been to Chepstow it's a lovely little market town with lots of riverside (Wye) pubs. But the River Severn is a beast of a river. Apparently, the tidal flow under the bridge is the second fastest in the world at spring tide time and between a high tide and low tide (six hours) the river will rise or fall as much as 50 feet. This creates deathly currents and at it's peak the water rushes up the river so fast that it creates a backwash that can, and is, literally surfed down. At any time, if you were to put a boat in the water and not attend to it, then it would have disappeared from sight in a minute or two.

Somehow I managed to reverse the car down the slipway and immerse the trailer in the river to a point that the boat simply floated off. I unhooked the boat from the trailer and, with the bow rope, managed to pull it around to the sheltered (from the current) side of the slipway. My mother held on to the bow rope while I drove back up the slipway and parked the car. I came back, clambered aboard and carried out my final checks (switched it on and turned the radio on). When ready, I engaged neutral (boats have forward, neutral and reverse) and started the engine. I took the bow rope from my Mum, engaged forward and slowly edged out into the open river. At this point the river is vast, at least two miles across and I could feel the current of the incoming tide pulling me quickly up river. I knew I had to allow the engine to warm up before hitting the power and when I was confident that it had, I jammed the throttle fully forward. The bow leapt into the air leaving me looking at clear blue sky but I knew that once the power had fully transferred to the propeller then the bow would drop down and I would be fully 'on the plane'. But it didn't and I remained pointing directly at the sky. It was very disconcerting. I pulled the throttle back, crashed down and tried again but the same thing happened, and again, and again. I then had a thought that maybe I hadn't released the pin that kept the outboard motor locked down for travelling. I went to the back of the boat, knelt on the back seats and reached down into the water to check the pin was out. It was, but I felt water on my knees and when I looked down I was aghast to see the back of the boat filling up with water very fast, I was sinking!

In my haste I hadn't put the drain plug in before launching and now, in a state of panic, it didn't occur to me to get it out of the glovebox, screw it in and then pump the water out. My immediate reaction was to get to land as quickly as possible. I put the throttle on full power – which had the boat pointing skyward at about 45° – and headed just as quickly as possible to shore. Was the shore sandy? No. Was the shore pebbly? No. The shore was rocky but I had no choice and ran the boat up onto the beach resulting in numerous deep scratches to the front third and underside as well as totally ruining the propeller. To say it was an embarrassing moment was an understatement. I got the plug in and a few amused onlookers pushed me back along to the slipway where I managed to get the car and trailer down and the boat out on to dry land. Only 30 minutes earlier I was launching a gleaming brand new boat into the water only to recover her with a mangled front end and underside. The repair was considerable; the embarrassment even more so!

The two years I spent in Bristol were quite brilliant. I had completely mastered my job and assembled a great team, to the point where I needed to do very little. My social life was great and I had two quite incredibly good summers. That meant there was lots of use of the boat –

and more 'amusing' incidents.

It's normal safety routine to have two people in a boat when towing a water skier: one to drive and look forward and the other to keep an eye on the skier (look backwards). But on one particularly hot and sunny day, there was just myself and Andy Pickard. Andy wasn't a great skier, nor did he have any experience of driving boats. But I was becoming a really quite competent mono skier and as it was such a fine day I asked him to drive and we would dispense with the third man. There were plenty of nice pubs along the riverbank whose gardens were brimming with people on such a fine summer afternoon. Of course, we attracted a lot of attention and as we sped up and down I was able to send up huge water 'roosters' as I cut back and forward. I got more and more adventurous and skied closer and closer to the bank until I made the mistake of getting so close that the fin on the underside of the ski caught in the soggy mud, ripping the ski off my foot and catapulting me 20 feet in the air. Thankfully, the banks of the Wye are not rocky, they are pure, soft, black stinking mud and I came down face first, with a huge squelch, at the bottom of a particularly packed beer garden. I arose like a beast emerging from a swamp, up to my knees in shit and unable to move, all to rapturous applause. In the meantime Andy, totally oblivious to my predicament was now half a mile away heading up river towards Tintern or Monmouth. All I could do was stand there and be ridiculed. Andy did eventually return and managed to drag me out of my soggy demise. After that experience I made sure that I kept securely in mid stream and always with a third man.

Once recovered and cleaned up we went back to skiing. There had been quite bad flooding up river a day or two before and I was happily skiing along when I suddenly spotted what appeared to be an upturned table in front of me. I saw it too late to take any avoiding action and so went straight over the top of it. Again I felt my fin stick and it wasn't until I had pretty well gone through it that the ski was pulled from my foot and off I came, taken downstream on the current with the table. Only it wasn't actually a table, but a dead pig – and a very bloated one. My fin had cut right through its stomach and the stench that emanated was dreadful.

As well as being enjoyable, my two years in Bristol were hugely rewarding and I achieved a lot. I had a nice home, enjoyed my boat immensely, did lots of partying and my branch was very successful. It was also the place where I first played golf (thanks to Andy) which, as anyone who knows me will know, became a great love of mine – even though I was never particularly good at it.

I was 29 and had been with the company for seven years when I got the call that really set me apart from the other (now) 130-odd branch managers. I was to be promoted to district manager. This would give me responsibility for about a dozen managers of branches from Ilford and Romford to the West up as far as

Norwich and Cambridge and all points between. At long last I would get a very decent pay rise and be able to trade my Ford Escort L for a very posh Ford Sierra Ghia. I had well and truly arrived!

7 - CRUISE CONTROL

I was promoted on the same day as two other managers: Dave Walton, from Reading and Dave Fretter from Nottingham. I knew them both a little as our three branches had historically been the platform for others to be promoted and so we all kept an eye on each other as we knew we were competing for the next promotion. But the company was growing so quickly, we were promoted together. We had to spend our first week at head office in Bracknell to be taught how to do the job. To be fair, it was even easier than the one we left and essentially meant visiting each branch four or or five times a year for three or four days each and making sure the manager was doing their job properly, following the guidelines. The highlights of that first week was taking delivery of the new car and spending most nights drinking far too much with Dave and Dave, using the 'work' days to recover. The two Daves became very good friends, but not without their ups and downs. I chose to lose contact with Dave Walton around 2015 but (apart from a nearly 20 year hiatus!) am still in touch with Dave Fretter.

I moved to the outskirts of Colchester and bought my third home, a three-bed bungalow in the village of Great Tey. I enjoyed my new job – it was a highly regarded position in the company and, given the culture was very much 'Command and Control', it allowed me to do pretty much what I pleased (within the constraints of a fairly tight set of rules). I didn't abuse the system and went about my work in a professional and diligent manner – well, to start with I did. In conducting my branch visits I had an operating manual, which told me down to the letter what I should do:

1. Arrive at branch, count cash (make sure it balanced with books).
2. Introduce myself to all staff.
3. Interview manager and get their view on the branch performance.
4. Review 10 recently made loans.
5. Review 10 overdue account files.
6. Etc, etc.

It was fairly humdrum and, once I had sorted out a few bad apples and got a good team around me, life became very easy. I quickly gave up following process and my branch visits really only involved chatting to the staff, making sure they were happy, geeing them up a bit and talking on the phone to Dave and Dave. The one danger area was that my boss (Mr Baines, I wasn't allowed to call him Kevin because it was against company policy to address senior management by their first name) would show up unannounced every two or three months to make sure I was doing my job properly. I soon discovered that either he wasn't very good at his job or he was as disinterested as I was in following procedure, so it became something of a sham. As long as I appeared to be doing what I was supposed to that was good enough.

As the company became more liberal – and living with an unmarried partner, growing a beard and being gay became acceptable to our lords and masters in Chicago – Mr Baines informed me that I could now call him Kevin. I asked him why and he replied 'because that's my name'. I offered my thanks but said that I preferred to call him Mr Baines and so it remained.

It was around this time that I met Paul Singer. Paul was a lawyer in Southend and we used his firm for some bad debt and legal work. He wasn't a typical lawyer, very down to earth and pragmatic, easy to relate to and he understood our business needs well. Paul is a bit like a Duracell bunny and just keeps going and going, he's always coming up with ideas and most of them are brilliant. He set up a very slick automated debt recovery area at the offices of his firm and we got some good results. That endeared me to him and we have stayed friends since. More than once I thought he and I might go into business together and had it not been for the fact the one or both of us were successful in what we were doing at the time then I think that really could have happened.

One of the very big perks of being a district manager at HFC was that all employees at that level and above attended a global conference every spring at a fancy resort in the US. My first one was in 1984 at a very smart golf and tennis resort in Florida: Saddlebrook. It was my first trip to the US and Dave, Dave and I stuck together as we were all a little overawed. There were nearly 1,500 attendees from all over the world and we were, of course, among the most junior. In fact, we had to identify ourselves at the gala reception as first-time attendees.

After all the speeches were made at the reception, we were let loose in an enormous marquee filled with free drinks and mountains of food. There were drinks carts set up all over the place and we tried a few before I discovered one where the bartender seemed to be serving extraordinarily large screwdrivers, which had immediately become my drink of choice. So our little group parked ourselves up against her bar and basically made it our own. Her name was Carol, a very attractive and bubbly blonde who I discovered was about four years younger than me and this work was helping her fund her studies at the nearby University of South Florida. We hit it off and I made a point of bumping into her every night of the six nights we were there. The first morning of the conference was a packed hall and the usual humdrum speeches from a procession of senior management, complete with lots of back slapping and self appreciation. The business meetings were held in the mornings and the afternoons were free time. Each evening there was some sort of organised event or dinner (coaches took random groups to pre-booked restaurants). I recall we only went to the first day meeting and figured with 1,500 people nobody would miss us so we didn't go again. Apparently by the last day the 1,500 had shrunk to about 800!

The conference was finishing on Friday morning and we had free time on Thursday night and one of the Dave's boss (Mr Collins, a particularly unlikeable thug-like north Londoner) decided that he was going to host a party in his room. Actually, it wasn't a room, but an enormous suite, with giant terrace. He instructed another junior colleague of ours (Russell) to wander around the pool on the Wednesday afternoon and recruit as many attendees as he could. If they wanted to attend then they were to give him a $20 contribution for booze and then Russell was to drive to the nearest town and buy as much as he could. The mandatory dress code for the party was one sock, a dressing gown and a hat, I've no idea why, I was merely a spectator. I'm not sure Mr Collins realised how persistent Russell was. He spent the entire afternoon pestering everyone and, by the time he had finished, he had collected well over $2,000 and gaily went into town. I think he cleaned out the entire store. We helped him unload and I swear I had never seen so much booze in one place. We didn't go to the party but the next morning Dave Fretter got a call from Mr Collins saying if he wanted any booze then to come up and help himself. Dave and I had long planned to spend an extra few days in Florida and were driving down to Fort Lauderdale for their infamous 'Spring Break' extravaganza. I can't quite recall how we got it – maybe from one of the many hotel kitchens – but we managed to snaffle a huge polystyrene chest, which we lined with six large bags of ice and wedged it into the back seat of our large, ugly and very gas thirsty Chevrolet sedan that we had rented. We managed to get about a year's worth of booze in and headed off to Fort Lauderdale, a four hour drive to the south.

I remember arriving in Fort Lauderdale in the early afternoon and we were totally mesmerised by the partying go on. Everywhere we looked, we were faced with a sea of drunken youths, most of whom were wearing hardly a jot. It was pure debauchery! We didn't really join in but parked up, found a bar that just happened to have the obligatory round the clock wet T-shirt contests and just sat and watched. It was a bizarre experience. We returned to our car after a couple of hours to find the whole of the back completely soaked from the melted ice – and all the booze approaching boiling point. We made the strategic decision to jettison it all and hauled the huge chest out, left it kerbside in the confident knowledge that every drop would be consumed.

We checked into our hotel and, while getting ready for the evening, I had a phone call from Carol to check we had made it and get my thoughts on Fort Lauderdale. I don't recall how it came up, but she had a couple of days off and, by the end of the call, it was agreed she would fly down the following morning and show us how to manage ourselves (even though I was 29, I was considerably out of my depth). She said she would get herself a hotel room for one night, but I assumed that might not be the case. Dave was less than pleased and I remember protesting my innocence and trying to convince him this was all very positive for both of us and we would benefit from her guidance. He wouldn't have it and, although we managed ourselves OK through the next 48 hours, his argument wasn't lost on me in the slightest.

A romance followed with Carol, but with her 'there' and me 'here', maintaining it was difficult. After a few months of phone calls and my visiting her home near Sarasota and meeting the family, we agreed that she would come and spend six months (the maximum allowed) in Essex with me. It wasn't to the liking of her mum (the boss of the household) but she wished us well and so it began. Carol couldn't work and so spent most of her time either studying or attending a variety of exercise classes, our relationship blossomed. When her visa expired after six months, she went back to Florida and we set our wedding plans. We married a few months later on the beach and with a small guest list of friends and family including (of course) Dave and Dave. Carol and I honeymooned in the

Bahamas where we visited the British Consulate where we had all the paperwork completed to allow her to return directly to the UK, visa free.

We got home to my little bungalow and things were really good. Carol managed to get herself a very good job on a trading desk of a large city investment bank and my job was going well too. Results were good and I had very little to do except keep things ticking along.

The work highlight of that following year was the next management conference, this time in Phoenix at a posh golf resort. I was now playing a little golf (badly) and so I was in my element. Dave and Dave didn't play but we met up in the evenings and partied hard as was the way at these things. Like the previous year, we decided to stay on for a few days after the conference and visit Las Vegas. Back in 1986 it wasn't like it is today, but it was still vast and all the hotels were incomparable to anything I had experienced before. We checked into ours (a small crummy place well away from the strip) and I'm not sure we actually saw the inside of the room much over the three nights we were there. I have no recollection of losing much money so, in that respect, the trip was a success! But I do remember that we had to get a flight at 07.00 from Phoenix to Washington, where we were picking up a connecting flight home. Given it's a four-hour drive we decided to leave Vegas sometime after midnight and travel through the night. The journey was uneventful until we hit Phoenix. At around 04.30 we pulled up at a set of lights in what appeared to be an area close to downtown. While waiting at the lights, a pick-up truck pulled up alongside. I glanced across and there were three Mexican-looking men in the front, but I didn't pay much attention. The lights went green and we drove the one block to the next lights, which had turned red. As we were waiting I noticed that the passenger of the truck, which was alongside us again, was trying to attract my attention. I wound my window down and he was holding a beer out and asking me if I wanted it. I guessed they were all drunk so I ignored them and then pulled away on the green light. At the next intersection, the same thing happened but this time I replied, saying that we didn't want his beer, to which he replied: "Are you ******** faggots?" I could see he was becoming more and more aggressive, which freaked us a bit. So, at the next lights, instead of going straight on I turned right at the last second and was relieved to see them heading straight on. At the next lights I turned left so we were running parallel with the road we were originally on. But as I went through the next set of lights, I saw the Mexicans had taken their next right and then turned left and were literally chasing after me. It was like a scene from a movie! At the next lights I flung the car right at the last second put my foot on the gas and took a random, right, left, right set of turns at the next few lights, all while driving at speeds of up to 60mph. Finally, I was happy that we had shaken them off but the next thing I see is blue flashing lights in my mirror followed by blue flashing lights in front of me with police cars blocking my way.

Naturally, I pulled over and got out of the car, before

I was quickly told to get back inside. I did so and a policeman came to the window, gestured to me to wind it down and asked for my licence. I fumbled around and found it but he clearly wasn't familiar with a UK licence so told me to get out of the car, move to the rear and spread my legs. I was then fully and robustly frisked and breathalysed. Throughout this ordeal, I was trying to explain that we felt endangered, but they showed no interest in listening to my story. Seemingly I was also driving the wrong way up a one way street and at speeds well in excess of the limit. They eventually instructed me to get back in the car and they went to their cars and talked it through. After what seemed like an eternity they returned and gave me a warning and thankfully no ticket.

By now we were ridiculously late for our flight and had just a few minutes to make check-in, but I knew I couldn't go faster than the speed limit. We were two miles from the airport and the roads were near empty. We got to the airport only to see the car rental return area was a good half mile from the terminal, so we decided to dump the car outside the terminal in a 'no parking' area, dash in, check our bags and leave the keys with a very confused check-in agent. We only just made our flight and, unbelievably, never heard a thing from the car rental company.

Later that year Carol and I decided to move from my little bungalow and we found a new five-bedroom house in Kelvedon, a smallish village between Colchester and

Chelmsford. It was in the process of being built and due to be finished four months later. The house was on a small development of just six properties a stone's throw from the high street. It was a high-quality house and cost us £99,950 – how times (and prices) have changed! We exchanged contracts fairly quickly and completion was set for three months later. House number four purchased.

Not long after signing for the house, and to my great surprise I got a phone call from a headhunter, I had never had one before. He introduced himself and told me he had an opportunity with American Express, just outside of Brighton as director in a division that was responsible for banking services and high value loans to the 'Gold' card customer base. I was ill-prepared for the call and, as it came on a Sunday night, I told him that unfortunately I had company, and we arranged for him to call me back the next day. The delaying tactic gave me a little time to prepare and figure out how I could best describe my career, achievements and suitability. He called back the next day, by which time I was fully prepared, with post-it notes all over the wall, ready for what turned out to be a half-hour introduction. A further three interviews were conducted over the next six weeks and eventually I got a call (again on a Sunday night) to tell me I had been successful. The headhunter went through the pay and benefits, which were a huge upgrade to what I was getting – but more important to me was the type of job and the business I would be joining, set up for life might be an overstatement but I had definitely moved from one of the lower leagues to the Premier league. I accepted without hesitation and the next morning I called my boss and gave my one month's notice. He was shocked, for no other reason than people at my level never resigned from the business, nobody ever had. Some were fired, but nobody had ever actually quit the firm. He called me back later in the day and told me to visit head office the next day at 4.00pm to see his boss, the vice president. I drove over to be lectured with his view that my career progression at HFC would be far better, that I was highly regarded and the sky was the limit yabba yabba yabba. He also told me that the American Express business model was not sustainable and that I would be moving into a world of insecurity. I showed the correct respect for his ridiculous comments but said that my mind was made up. His response to that was to tell me to hand over all my company property there and then, including my car keys. I asked him how I should get home and that I had a lot of personal stuff in the car, but he said that was my problem. So much for being highly regarded! As a result, I had to travel across London by train during rush hour, carrying my briefcase, golf clubs and an assortment of carrier bags – what an end to 11 years of loyal service! If I had any doubt I might have made the wrong decision I certainly didn't after that experience.

My new job was based in an office in Burgess Hill just north of Brighton where Amex had set up this new division nine months prior and had been testing various concepts. They were now launching and ramping up staff, hence my recruitment. Obviously I would need to move house from Essex but I was committed to buying the Kelvedon house, which wasn't due to be finished for another six weeks. I went back to the builder and asked him if he would do a deal with me and buy the house back. The property market was booming and I knew that if he were selling it now he could have got more than the £99,950 I had agreed to pay. But he actually offered me £5,000 less saying that the specification I had chosen for the bathrooms and kitchen might not be to everyone's taste. I knew he was trying to take advantage so I went to an estate agent in the village and asked for his opinion. He looked over the house and suggested I could get £130,000 and so I told him he could have the business. The very next day he called me and said I had been offered the full asking price by a cash buyer. The result meant that I actually completed on the purchase and sale on the same day six weeks later.

I also put my bungalow on the market and a month later we found ourselves in a very nice apartment in a block opposite the Marina in Brighton. Although a little apprehensive I was looking forward to my first day working for Amex. The year was 1986, I was 31 years old.

8 - SUCCESS AND FAILURE

There was no comparison between Amex and HFC. The former was highly professional, with scores and scores of highly educated and talented people. It just oozed quality. HFC was much more of a 'roll your sleeves up' kind of place with a random bunch of people with one thing in common: they all worked really hard. Amex was more about thinking hard, or that's how it liked to be thought of - intellectual leadership.

I had a small team to start with, 20 people and my first task was to recruit more. American Express wanted to pump a lot of money and marketing into the business over the following 18 months and the plan was for me to have upwards of 200 staff by the end of the following year. In the early days, I pulled out three people from HFC: Andy from Bristol; Mike Bowman, an assistant manager from Southend and Chris Fisher the branch manager from

Chelmsford. They were all good at their jobs and I was obviously familiar with them and most importantly knew I could rely on them to do a good job. I put them in as managers of the three biggest departments I had and they set about recruiting and establishing procedures and getting the systems requirements sorted out for IT. The customer proposition was absurdly attractive – a guaranteed £10,000 overdraft with American Express Bank at a rate of 2% over base when signing up for a gold card. We were being inundated.

I very soon alerted my boss, Robert Hallam, to the notion of arrears and bad debt. I don't think it was anything he really ever considered and I recall him telling me that Amex Cardholders were upscale, wealthy professionals and we should not be too concerned. Apart from all the operational areas that I managed (including credit control and collections, which was getting far too busy) I also had the risk and credit assessment functions. The tools they were using were very basic and it took time to build up the data to identify those who we should be declining for the product and my boss was not willing to put the brakes on our growth until he had empirical evidence to justify doing so. All the time the workload in credit control was rising, but the rapid growth of acquisition was masking a huge downstream problem (I had seen all of this before) which would come back to bite us. Months later, in a senior management meeting, Giuseppe Mancini, head of the business in Europe, openly humiliated my boss by saying: "Robert, there are three elements to running a business: growth; profit and control and I think you only understand one of those." Shortly after that meeting, Robert left the business. Ben East was the marketing director at the time and was promoted to take over the business. Thankfully Ben was more understanding of the impact of bad credit decisions than Robert and we started to put the brakes on what was very indiscriminate lending.

At home we spent four months in the apartment opposite the Marina before we bought our house, a fairly new and large 4 bedroom house in Rudgwick, some 20 miles north east of Burgess Hill on the road between Horsham and Guildford. Carol was able to use Gatwick Airport or Horsham for her commute to London and, while things were fine between us, work was consuming far too much of our time and we became like ships in the night.

I had sold my boat a couple of years earlier and now, with my new salary and feeling very comfortable, I was ready to buy another one. I had my eyes on a bigger boat manufactured by the US company, Bayliner. In the UK, the boat would have cost me £35,000, but I discovered that if I went to the US, I could buy it for about £20,000 and with shipping and import duty I would still save up to £8,000. I found a distributor just outside of Miami and basically bought the boat over the phone and arranged a date to go over, check it out and pay. After that, I organised the shipping and customs paperwork, and put everything in place.

I had made a few friends in the area courtesy of the landlord of the pub (Daryl) around the corner, who introduced me to a group of golfers, which helped me settle in quickly. After I had done the deal on the boat I mentioned it to Daryl, who told me he had an apartment in Miami Beach. He suggested we go over together and I could use his spare room to save me finding accommodation.

A month later we headed off to Florida and, on the first night, Daryl wanted to show me the delights of South Beach Miami. If you've never been, it's a very unique place – frequented by all sorts and Daryl knew some real dives. I particularly remember the Thunderbird Hotel. The bar was filled with people, none of whom looked under 60 and most looked, well, just weird. Daryl was quick to point out people he knew of, most of whom had strange names like Harry the Horse and Shotgun Lulu. According to Daryl, who was something of a story teller, the bar was known as a meeting place for 'retired' New York underworld types.

While sitting with our beer we were approached by a big elderly fella who Daryl knew and there was much hugging and back slapping. He introduced himself as GJ, or something like that. He talked – and looked like – an ageing (in those days) Sylvester Stallone. 'GJ' sat down and we went through the polite small talk and he asked me what I was doing over here. I told him about the boat and why I was buying it in the US. He then asked me how I was paying for it and I told him by Travellers

Cheques. He then propositioned me, offering me $15,000 in cash for my $30,000 of Travellers Cheques. Simple, I get $15,000 and report the cheques lost/stolen and get them replaced and my cheques simply 'disappear'. I didn't think too long before declining his generous offer but he was persistent and the longer I held out the more frustrated he became. Eventually, I managed to get out and, at that point, I was thankful that I was only staying a day or two in South Beach. Needless to say I didn't return to the Thunderbird, nor any other of the seedy establishments, during my short stay.

My boat arrived in Rudgwick two months later. As it was winter, I stored it safely in my garage, thankfully large enough for most of it to fit in. In the spring I booked it in for a first service and preparation (degreasing from the winter lay up) ready for the upcoming summer. I had just got a new company car on which I asked for a towbar to be fitted with a 2 inch fixing ball. There was a Bayliner dealer in Brighton and so I booked the boat in and towed it down one Friday morning and agreed to collect it the following morning. Everything went well with the delivery, no problems whatsoever towing the boat and dropping it at the dealer. I collected it as agreed on Saturday morning and, as I was heading out of Brighton, not far from the seafront on the A23 London Road the road dipped - like an upside down hump. As I came out the other side I felt a lurch and then, a few seconds later, I saw that my trailer had detached from the towbar and was actually overtaking me! I was horrified and completely powerless. The boat went past me and hit an island in the middle of the road, redirecting it across the front of me and now heading for a junction on the left and beyond – straight for a large Sainsbury's. As it approached the pavement, at a fair speed too, a lady looked up and put her arms out as if to try and stop it. Now this boat and trailer weighed around 1,000lbs and it would have run right across her and most likely killed her. Thank goodness on the corner of the junction there was a crash barrier and it did its job bringing the boat to a stop just inches from her.

I pulled over and got out of the car in total shock, probably the first time in my life I had experienced such a feeling – and it's impossible to describe. I was all but incoherent and could hardly stand up, indeed a passer by got me to sit down just before I was violently sick. I don't recall much after that. The police were there quickly and the AA took the boat off to the police compound. I do remember thinking that I must be cursed, given that I'd owned two brand new boats, both of which suffered extensive damage before even being used!

To add insult to injury, when I arrived at work on Monday morning I discovered I had made headline news in the Evening Argus. The paper really had gone to town, with a full front page dedicated to the accident, a large photograph and a variety of eye witness accounts. More boat-related embarrassment for me!

It was sometime later that I discovered the cause of the accident. When ordering my car, I also ordered a 2 inch towball to be fitted but, as everything had now converted to metric, the dealer decided to fit the nearest size they had, which was 50mm and which meant it didn't lock properly. I'm not sure why I didn't sue the dealership for the cost of the repair! I also got eight penalty points on my licence, four for having an unroadworthy car/trailer and four for not having orange indicators on the trailer (they were red as was the norm in the US at the time).

The boat was eventually repaired and restored to its original condition and I decided to buy a mooring in Brighton Marina. From then on I had a great two years or so with the boat - skiing, fishing and just generally enjoying being in and around the sea.

Things with Carol were OK, and although work was consuming a lot of our time it was probably no more so than lots of couples at our stage of life. I guess its what happens as you build a life, a home and prepare for the future. But I was so focussed on my job and knew that I had a really good opportunity to set myself up for life.

The business was developing well and we had recruited scores of people, so much so that I was asked to take the lead in finding and moving to new offices as we had no space left in our building. I found something less than half a mile away and my boss gave me an absurdly high budget to fit it out. He told me he wanted to showcase our business to the rest of the Amex world and to spend whatever it took. So I did and the result was really quite magnificent. The building was much bigger than we were leaving, with room for up to 700 staff when, at the time, we had 300.

It was during this time that my Mum died. She went quickly, painlessly and without warning. I was saddened by her passing, of course, and it took me a while to get over it. Indeed I was probably in shock for the second time in my life, so much so that I went into work the day after she died and recall being as useless as a chocolate teapot. Someone eventually told me to go home and I went and looked after Peter for a day or two as quite naturally he was struggling to come to terms with it too.

My secretary (Briony) offered her condolences and wanted to do whatever she could to help me through the period immediately after. I don't know if that made me vulnerable (probably not) but I got the sense that she was attracted to me and it caused me considerable issues. Some weeks later Carol was heading off to Florida for two weeks to visit her family and, a day or two after she left, the inevitable (as was becoming clearer to me) happened when I invited Briony to lunch. The rest, as they say, is history and a short affair of a few days followed. I really have no idea why I did it. Carol returned from holiday after two weeks but the day before she did, Briony put a note through my letterbox telling me how much she enjoyed being around me and that she thought she was falling in love. I tore the letter into pieces, threw it in the rubbish and just wished I could wind the clock back a week. I had screwed up and knew it, no blame whatsoever on Briony, it was all of my making.

Carol got back and all was normal but when I got home from work the next day, she was waiting for me and clearly furious. She had found the letter in the rubbish and pieced it together and we had a huge argument. The bottom line was that I was to fire Briony straight away and that was the condition she set for us to put things right. Now, Briony was a divorced mother of two young children and I couldn't do it. I told Carol that this was my fault and that I would find myself another job immediately but she wouldn't have any of it. She was adamant that I had to fire Briony and to do so right away. No matter how much I protested and offered alternatives, including quitting immediately myself, it wasn't acceptable to her. Three days later she was gone and, while I attempted to meet with her and patch things up, we couldn't make it work. I did try and find another job but I think it was half-hearted and therefore unsuccessful. When I reflect on that period it was quite obvious that I wasn't ready for marriage, firstly I was still growing up from an emotional perspective and secondly I was so consumed by my work that I didn't have the capacity to focus on the things that should have been more important to me. But, I had to dust myself down and I did.

We divorced about a year later and, in order to settle

matters financially, the house was sold. I found a new house (number five) and moved to Hove, a very nice older three-bedroom property in one of the best parts near Hove Park. Shortly after that I received a fairly decent promotion at work and moved down to Brighton to work in the main card business as director of operations. I was now at the very heart of the UK business, with responsibility for the largest staff group in the country – 600 employees.

I did quite a lot of improvements on the house, refitting kitchens and bathrooms as well as adding an extension to provide a fourth bedroom. I settled well into my new job and had a great team around me, which made for a good working life. I got on well with my peers and boss and everything was going well. I put my failed marriage behind me as best I could, but frequently regretted my actions – particularly when home alone and with time on my hands.

My new boss was Martin Augier and probably one of the two or three most impressive people I have ever worked for. He taught me so much, he was a superb leader and commanded the respect of everyone around him. He was decisive, prepared to take (calculated) risks and had a detailed understanding of every part of the business. I took a lot of his learnings and applied them to my own business units with great success and I knew my work wasn't going unnoticed.

Some time after moving to Brighton one of the ladies that worked for me suggested that I meet up with one of her friends and play squash as she was a keen player too. After a while, I agreed and that was how I met Dele. She was bright and bubbly and very sociable and fun and we saw each other for about two years during which time she moved into the house and things became fairly serious.

I thoroughly enjoyed my work. The people were good and the backup and systems were first class - it would have been very difficult to fail. I pulled a couple of people in from the previous job - to run the collections and new accounts departments - and I introduced 24/7 working across several departments. That initiative was very successful and earned me some good recognition.

However, it wasn't all plain sailing. One particularly difficult situation I got myself into was when one of the authorisations managers came to me because a cardholder called Sheikh something or other was trying to put a charge through for around £5,000 to a Paris hotel and he was already overdue by nearly a month for £10,000. We had numerous Arab Sheikh cardholders and they could be awkward and unreliable. In many cases we never really knew if they were actually a Sheikh and if so how far up the royalty line they were. Certainly if we declined the charge we would have difficulty getting any of our money back and if we approved it and he still didn't pay we have knowingly added to the problem. I approved the charge but asked that the Sheikh's PA contact me to tell me when he planned to pay. Thankfully I heard from her (Miss Simmons) a few days later telling me that he had a significant sum in US Dollars to exchange to British Pounds and would be doing so in the next few days, once the exchange rate had recovered. She insisted that I must let him continue using his card so that his honour wasn't compromised. Two weeks later and his balance had risen to over £20,000 and I get to talk to her again and she fed me the same story. Fast forward four months and he now owed close to £80,000 and my boss was warning me of the severe implications if I had got this wrong. I feared the worst, even though I was talking to Miss Simmons almost daily and being given the same reassurances, which I didn't believe one bit.

Then, one day I get a call from the reception desk at Amex House saying that there is a Miss Simmons to see me! I rush down and she is in reception along with a huge black man in chauffeur uniform (I spotted a large, new Mercedes in the visitor parking out front). She hands over an envelope with a draft for over £100,000, plus a very large box, which she says is for me for all my help. I take it all back to my office - stopping off at the cashiers on the way up - and open the box. Inside were 10 boxes of handmade Harrods chocolates, a dozen Harrods silk ties, 10 Harrods vouchers for £200 each and a Rolex watch (not fake!). I took it to my boss and asked him what I should do with it and he asked me what I wanted to do with it. I told him that I would like to keep the Rolex and raffle the rest among the Credit Control departments and give the money raised to a local hospice. Very surprisingly, he agreed. I'm not even sure the Rolex compensated for the stress I had endured for the previous six months, but it could've been a whole lot worse. I immediately closed the account of the Sheikh and opened a '45' account which was billed in US$ and thankfully that area wasn't my responsibility.

It was during this time that I developed a keen interest in cars and decided that one day I would own a Ferrari. But, as a not particularly well off 32-year-old, that time wasn't now, so I started out with a Lotus Espirit. It was an iconic car of the era and one that had featured in a recent James Bond film, so had the right credentials. I chose one (second hand) in the colours of the Lotus Formula One team sponsor, JPS (black and gold) and it was the perfect introduction to the world of 'proper' sports cars. But, the build quality wasn't brilliant – well, actually it was absolutely terrible – and there were always niggly things going wrong. The most annoying problem was the amount of condensation that would get into the cabin, because of poorly fitting door seals. I had good times with the Lotus though, but after a year I replaced it with a real brute of a car: a Renault GTA V6 Turbo. It came in the most gorgeous pearlescent white that made it look like the inside of a shell in the sun. I'm surprised anyone was allowed to drive these cars without some kind of special licence. The power was incredible (at least compared with anything I had ever driven) and it was delivered in a real muscular way with a huge amount of turbo lag to contend with.

Imagine putting your foot down as the lights go green and nothing happens and then a nano second later you are literally catapulted forward. How I didn't rear end cars along Dyke Road is anyone's guess. It was a thrilling car – difficult to say if it was the best I ever owned but it is up there.

Every year Amex had a big thee-day conference for senior management across Europe and the second one I attended was in Amsterdam, my first-ever visit to the city. Amex really knew how to do things well and we had our gala dinner and speeches in the Diamond Exchange. It was a black tie affair and when dinner was over and people were mingling waiting for the speeches to start, Chris Fisher and another couple of fellas came across to me and suggested we go downstairs to the toilet and roll a spliff. It might sound unbelievable but I had never ever got anywhere near any kind of drug, apart from paracetamol! I don't really know why, it had never even occurred to me I suppose. Anyway, we went down and we rolled what looked to me like a huge one and we stood in a cubicle passing this giant joint between us. Goodness knows what we were thinking, if we had been caught it would have been the end of our careers right there and then. I wasn't at all prepared for what hit me. I am told that the hash in Amsterdam is 'as good as it gets' and this stuff really went to town on me. The others seemed perfectly OK, but I was laughing uncontrollably, and about nothing! My imagination was running riot and I had lost pretty much all control of most of my functions. This was a real problem! We had to get back to the main auditorium or we would be missed and that wasn't clever. Less clever was me trying to get back upstairs, but somehow I managed it and the story was going to be I had drunk too much. But I'd never seen anyone behave that way on too much drink. We took our places as far back and as far to the side as we could while one of the country heads was running through the annual results. I don't know how long it lasted, but everything was amusing me and goodness knows how I managed to control myself, but I did. I drank copious amounts of water and, after what seemed like an eternity, I felt myself returning to normal, I had dodged career annihilation by a whisker.

Once the speeches were over there was the predictable mingling/networking and a group of us were approached by half a dozen of the senior ladies. They knew we were the adventurous types and they asked if we would take them to see a sex show. It was certainly more appealing than trying to come up with interesting chat with the Spanish Finance Director, so we agreed and headed off to the red light district. We just wandered in to one of the first places we came across, a poorly lit and fairly small room with a very brightly lit stage. There were about 60 wooden seats laid out in about eight rows and I guess about three people watching what was going on. Up on the stage, a man and woman were in a situation I can only describe as primitive - it was quite revolting to me and I've truly never been into anything like that.

There was a small bar at the back and I told the women and the other men to sit down while I got the drinks. I went to the bar and ordered four pints, three gin and tonics and three glasses of wine. The barman got halfway through the drinks, muttered something and disappeared. I turned to look at the stage and the aforementioned couple were finishing their act and walking off to no real applause (do you even applaud that sort of thing?). I turned back to the bar and my man still hadn't returned. I was conscious of activity on the stage, so turned back and was horrified to see the barman walking on (in nothing more than a G string) with an equally unclad girl. Oh my God! But that wasn't the worst of it. The girl who had been up on the stage when we arrived now came through the side door of the bar and asked me what the order was and that she would finish it. I'm not sure what I said, but I did get the drinks, distributed them to the group and left, Ugh!

After about two years in my new job, my boss called me into his office to tell me a new vice president position had been created in the old business I'd left and I was being asked to apply for it. It was still reporting to the managing director, but combined all of operations and risk management, a few other back office functions as well as the P&L responsibility for the new credit card that American Express was about to launch, the first anywhere in the world outside of the US. Accepting the job (assuming it was offered) would put me on the UK management committee for Amex and, at 34, I would become the youngest ever VP in the UK company. It didn't take any thinking and when offered the job, I accepted it in a heartbeat. Unfortunately that was the beginning of the end.

It was early 1990 and the country was going through a tough economic period. I was prepared for issues in my new job and my boss had explained how bad debt was rising. But I wasn't prepared for what I ran into at all. The almost indiscriminate lending that I found when I first arrived in 1986 – and had put a stop to – had started all over again. Not only were the bad debt numbers high (something I was prepared for) but there was an avalanche of bad business that was still classified as current and up-to-date, but it didn't need a rocket scientist to see where it was headed. Huge amounts of people using their £10,000 overdrafts to support excessive lifestyles and able to make monthly repayments by simply drawing it down from their overdraft. The 'Risk' people had been warning both marketing and the CEO of what was happening, but their warnings had been ignored. We tried all sorts of things – ramping up staff to deal with the deluge of bad business and cutting off new business by well over a half to try and stem the tide. I recall the pressure cooker environment and just how difficult it was to recover. Losses were mounting and would continue to mount as more bad business flowed through. I communicated, as far up the management line as I could, the likelihood that considerably more money than was going to be needed to write this business off to bad debt.

If you're going to fall out with anyone in a business then, apart from your boss, don't do so with the HR director. Although junior to me, Rona Fleetwood was very well connected and a typical HR schmoozer. I had little time for her and she knew it. In terms of my work, I had a fire-fight on my hands but she completely ignored that and was forever putting obstacles (people, recruiting, irrelevant training) in my way and it caused tension and prevented me from doing my job as effectively as I could. I knew my hostilities with her put me at risk as did the continuing poor business results. But we did eventually begin to see a slowdown in the deterioration but, if it weren't for Rona and her distractions, we could have got there a whole lot quicker.

As a consequence of the tensions and the danger it represented, I paid more attention to the frequent headhunter calls I received. One in particular caught my attention, head of sales and marketing with Avco, a business much along the lines of my first employer, HFC. It was smaller and 'rougher around the edges' and it certainly needed a more 'intelligent' way of operating. I met with the MD and was impressed by his desire to introduce quite radical change. He needed people from 'the outside' to help him drive the change and he told me that his intention was that I would succeed him one day. It was interesting but I wasn't completely sold. Although I promised to give it some thought, I knew I wasn't going to quit Amex to take the job.

Pretty well immediately after meeting Avco, Ben called me into his office and when I went in Rona was sat there with 'that look' on her face. I knew immediately something was wrong. Ben skirted around things; how much he appreciated all the good work I was doing, how things were on the mend, etc. He then went on to say that I was being offered a role in strategic planning in New York. I thanked him for the kind words and offer but said that I was happy in my current role and had no desire to relocate. He went on to tell me that it was what everyone wanted for me and that he strongly urged me to accept. I then knew for sure where this was going and I got the answer I feared which was that rejecting the offer wasn't really an option for me. If I didn't want to take it, the company would put together a very generous severance package. I knew from the way Amex worked that there was no point in protesting. Rona had inveigled up the chain of command - probably over months - and my destiny had been determined well before that meeting. I am sure the terms of the severance were on her desk right then. They did agree to give me a week to think it through, which was something. However, the moment I got back to my office, I called the headhunter with the Avco job and told him to let them know I was very interested. It happened quickly and less than two weeks later I had a written offer for a job at its head office in Reading. The role was broadly the same salary and benefits I was getting at Amex and I accepted the offer. When I went back to Ben and Rona and told them I wasn't going to accept their offer, Rona went to her office and returned not two minutes later with a letter offering me one year's salary and bonus. I put on a bit of an act of protest but accepted their terms and signed the deal. Just like that she asked for my pass and called security for them to accompany me to my office and clear my things. Some 15 minutes later I was in my car driving home, totally undignified and a horrid end to what had been a very prosperous and successful five years.

It was 1991, inflation was rampant and mortgage rates were at 13 or 14%. On top of that a big tax break (MIRAS) had been reformed and the housing market was flat dead, but I had to put my house on the market and move. Avco gave me an apartment in Reading for six months so that bought me some time, but not nearly enough to avoid what turned out to be a hefty loss on the Hove house.

While my work life was as successful as I could hope for, my ability, or perhaps desire, to forge a successful personal relationship was still a long way off. I enjoyed being with and around Dele but I couldn't make a permanent commitment, even though she was a lovely lady. Moving job and needing to relocate forced the issue and neither of us were confident that her moving up to Berkshire with me was sensible, so we mutually agreed to part. Very oddly I bumped into her some 20 years later when attending the first Brighton and Hove Albion game at the club's new stadium, which is, ironically, sponsored by American Express. Even more odd was that she was also a season ticket holder and her seat was only about five along from mine. We exchanged hello's and small talk and I guess we both got used to it.

My leaving American Express was the cause of the biggest financial disaster of my life, by a long stretch. so, if you're reading this book for a laugh, look away now!

On leaving the business and, as a senior executive and officer of the business, I was entitled to specialist financial advice in respect to my pension and the options available to me. I was set up to meet a couple of very slick financial advisers from a huge worldwide firm with an enviable reputation. They brought with them detailed calculations of my pension situation and recommendations. Essentially my combined American Express and HFC pensions would provide me an income of £40,000 annually when I reached 60. It would then grow at the rate of inflation - or 3-5% - and there would be a widows pension, too. But, if I transferred out into a private pension then at rates equivalent to what equities markets had returned in the previous 10 years, I would get nearly £80,000 annually. Even if the returns underperformed the market rates by as much as 30% I would still get £60,000. They presented swathes of data and it was a simple decision, I transferred out of the final salary schemes and the money was invested in an Aviva with profits bond. I forgot about it and got on with life.

Some 10 years later I received a letter from the Financial Regulator saying I might be among a small group (the practice of transferring pensions in such a way was only started about six months before I did mine and was stopped about 18 months later as it needed a lot more governance and regulatory oversight) of people who were inappropriately advised. I took a long hard look at the returns of the preceding 10 years and it was immediately apparent that they were way off what had been suggested. Indeed they were so pitiful that even a simple calculation showed that I would only be receiving the minimum that Aviva guaranteed which was £7,000 annually and no inflationary increases either (something I had missed). I submitted my mis-selling claim to the regulator and it was about six months before I heard that they had found in my favour - hooray! To compensate me they had instructed the financial advisory firm to pay a further £18,000 into my pension fund - boo!

I appealed to the regulator, arguing that it was a paltry sum and nowhere near what was needed. My rough calculations got me closer to £250,000 and even then the ongoing performance of the investments would need to improve radically. I got nowhere and was basically told that I wasn't qualified to make such calculations and they had an army of actuaries going over what was needed. They argued that their calculations showed that my fund would increase in value sufficiently to buy me a £40,000 pension at age 60 and that I had no evidence to prove them wrong. That bit was true, for sure, but you'd have to be a halfwit to buy that story. It was utter nonsense and I suspect politically motivated by the financial industry, as proper compensation could have ruined many of the firms. I was told that if I did not sign to accept the offer then I would receive no compensation at all. After months of protesting I reluctantly signed and hoped that investment returns would improve. They never did.

In my early 50s I took the matter up again as I was now nearing 60 I had the evidence that I didn't have 20 years earlier - my pension was shot to bits. I got absolutely nowhere, the regulator shrugged it off because I had signed the acceptance, even though it was under duress. I took the matter to my MP - who was sympathetic but useless - and I even went to the European Court of Human Rights as two of my core, fundamental rights had been violated (Article 17 - The right to peaceful ownership of my property, it cannot be taken away without good cause and Article 8 - The right to remedy). It was a long and drawn out process and it will probably come as no surprise that my claim was rejected on the basis that I hadn't exhausted the judicial system in my own country. The simple reason for that was cost, I simply couldn't afford to.

By the time I was 55 I calculated that I needed my fund increased by about £1.7m to provide me with the pension I was entitled to. I looked long and hard for a top draw city law firm to take on my case on a 'no win no fee' basis and I eventually found one - hooray! But there was a catch. They would take 25% of anything I won. It was a lot of money, but I was OK with that. But, they then told me that if I were to win (as they thought very possible) then the publicity that the case would get would open the floodgates to a large number of claims of the same type. The firm warned me that the defendants (the firm of advisers and the financial regulator) would throw everything at their defence. If I were to lose then I would have to pay their costs, which they said could be several millions of pounds. Naturally I couldn't take the risk - boo!

However, about a week later, the law firm called me back saying they had found a Lloyds Insurance broker who had looked at my case and was willing to insure me against any loss in the event I lost the case - hooray! But there was a premium to pay, of course. I asked how much and they told me £400,000 - boo! But I did give it serious thought, I wasn't sure how I would raise that kind of money but I didn't immediately dismiss it. Ultimately I did, of course, and here I am today with a crap pension. Thankfully Judy and I were able to squirrel enough away to ensure we/she won't be living in poverty in old age.

Even as I write this the injustice of it pains me greatly. I've long held the belief that 'money is the root of all evil' and here was a stark reminder, if ever I needed one. If I ruled the world I would have it so that wealth was measured and accumulated by the degree to which one displayed and demonstrated goodwill. I don't know where I'd sit in that class system but I sure as hell know we would all be a lot happier!

9 - WORK, OR WAS IT PLAY?

To say that Avco was a culture shock would be a massive understatement, and it didn't start well either. Martin Woodhouse (the MD and my boss) invited me to dinner at Wentworth golf club with his management team on the Sunday night before my first day. I had met one of them (Lorren Wyatt, VP HR), but not the others, so we went around the table and I was introduced to: Rob Plumb (VP, finance – seemed like a pleasant guy); Simon Terry (VP Operations – seemed to sneer at me and was hostile from the off); Richard Robson (VP, IT – middle-aged geek) and, finally, Paul Carson, who was also starting the following day. Paul was going to be working for me, developing a new strategy for broker-introduced lending business. This news immediately sent alarm bells ringing because Martin had previously told me my first objective was to look at how we worked as a business in respect to products, channels, marketing effectiveness and business sourcing. But it appeared he had already made some decisions himself and was going ahead regardless. On top of that, I took an instant dislike to Paul. He was totally old school, a lifetime in sub-prime finance and a close friend of Martin, which he made sure wasn't lost on me. Paul was also keen to point out that he had already arranged a weekly update with Martin to appraise him of progress. I intended to put a stop to that right away.

I arrived the next day and met with Martin in his office on the fourth floor – the Exec floor of a very badly designed building, with a huge centre lift shaft core, which made the rest of the floorspace really narrow. Thankfully, I was on the first floor with my team, which suited me well. Interestingly, though, Paul's office was on the fourth floor. Martin and I went through the small talk and I confronted him about the Paul situation, basically telling him I wasn't comfortable with him working for me. I didn't know if broker-introduced business was going to be material in the strategy I would be developing and it was clear that he and Paul wanted to work closely together. Martin's resistance was that Paul was 'only' an assistant VP and wasn't at a level that should be reporting to him, which had zero merit in my world. I stuck to my guns and adopted a 'start as you mean to go on' approach. Martin eventually agreed (I later discovered he agreed to most things) but said that he wouldn't make it public. That suited me, so I didn't have to deal with Paul, who I quickly discovered was stuck in a 1970's time warp.

After leaving Martin, I walked my floor and met my team one by one. I didn't expect an abundance of MBAs and highly educated graduates keen to impress, but I was in for a bit of a shock. Most of them had found themselves in sales and marketing by chance, either transferred in from other functions or recruited externally without any real due diligence. I don't think anyone had any professional qualification. However, I detected a very strong desire to do a good job and real enthusiasm across the entire department. At the end of the day, those were the raw materials I needed and, despite the lack of experience in the team, I was optimistic. From a personality perspective I liked everyone, they seemed a decent group of people who appeared enthusiastic and all well aligned. I could work with that.

Almost immediately, I was confronted by two main challenges. Firstly, the whole approach to sales and marketing was wrong. Sales comprised four of five business development managers that the branches (operations) simply ignored. They were on a hiding to nothing, so that had to change. Secondly, the marketing effort was little more than home made, in-house creative and copy writing, which was then photocopied and sent to branches to post out in handwritten envelopes. It was embarrassing. On top of that, the branches ignored marketing as well and simply did their own thing. This situation was historic and born out of a sense that "the branch was king and knew better than anyone". The fact was, they knew very little and from what I could see the company survived on a very small shred of business that relied on turning over the same customers time and again, getting all their big interest payments before flipping them into larger loans and selling ancillary insurance with eye-watering premiums. With responsibility for branch operations, Simon Terry did as he pleased and, although he was my peer, he didn't afford me or my function the slightest bit of respect. He ruled by fear and power, which meant none of the vast number of people who worked for him paid us any respect either. To cap it all, Martin was not a particularly robust leader and just turned a blind eye to everything. It only took a few days to realise that pretty much everything he told me in the interview in respect to my role and his plans for the future was little more than an idealogical dream. Something had to change and quick!

I knew of Avco from my time at HFC and one thing I knew was that they rarely, if ever, hired senior people from outside, everything was from within. I expected a fairly rough ride from the Operational areas and I knew I'd have to work hard to win their respect. The rump of the business operated in a command and control fashion and they worked hard (well perhaps) and played hard (very definitely). I was more likely to gain the respect I needed not by introducing new methods or initiatives, but by showing them that I could "mix it" with them. Fortunately the annual Managers conference was going ahead in central London about two weeks after I joined and so I volunteered myself to take the stage before dinner and introduce myself by giving them a light hearted talk. A year or two earlier I had the good fortune to be at an event where the after dinner speaker, David Gunson, gave an eye-wateringly funny account of life as an air traffic controller including describing flying Concorde from London to New York [I highly recommend you Google it and have a listen]. I had his story recorded and I decided to learn the entire thing, which took many hours, and I delivered my 20/25 minute adaptation of it to the 200 or so audience before dinner. I have no doubt that single event helped me immensely to win over many of those in the Operational areas. Unfortunately that didn't extend as far as Simon Terry and some of his immediate team but I knew I had made good progress with a large proportion of the front line Management.

Back in Hove, I was getting nowhere selling my house. I had paid £240,000 for it and spent at least another £40,000 extending and improving it. I think I started off on the market at £275,000 and eventually, over a year later, I sold it for £199,000. I recently looked it up online and two years ago it was sold for £1.1m. You win some, you lose some...

I quickly set about introducing as much change (as per my original brief) as best I could. I had convinced Martin to give me a substantial increase in budget to professionalise our approach, materials and hopefully reputation. One of the first things I did was call Harty back at Amex and offer him the job of running marketing. I felt a bit bad for Phil (Steel) who was running it as he was as keen as mustard, but we needed radical change. Phil understood that, plus I had other plans for him that would be much more suited to his skills and experience. Harty immediately rejected my offer and so I simply kept increasing the salary increments by £2,500 until he said yes. In fairness, there were other reasons for him giving it a go – he had a blank canvas to work with as opposed to operating in a very narrow track at Amex with little responsibility other than interacting with the agency. After he joined, we quickly started to improve the quality of the function.

The biggest, but totally expected, issue was getting any kind of traction with the branch operations. Simon was as close to a psychopath as I'd ever met and nobody would dare cross him. Despite knowing that I had gained credibility with many in the operation, I realised that everyone was petrified of Simon and it wasn't long before I started to think I had made a huge mistake and perhaps I should set about looking for another job. As fortune (I think!) would have it, Martin decided to resign and join a competitor. I had only been in the business for three months, but I put my name in the frame to lead the business, as did Simon and Rob. I wasn't expecting to be successful, but I wanted the opportunity to talk to the top brass in California and tell them what a dysfunctional business they had and what a huge obstacle Simon was to effecting change. Thankfully it worked and I had very good conversations as far up to the President of the entire business. He was obviously aware of Simon's behaviours and assured me that he would see that I got full support in introducing the much needed change into the business. In the end, Rob got the job, which was no surprise. He was intellectually strong and knew the business inside out. He also knew about the dangers of Simon but, unfortunately, he was a passive character and I doubted he would be able to actually influence Simon's behaviour in any way. Whilst I was correct in that thinking, Simon took not getting the MD's job pretty badly and spent a considerable amount of time 'pestering' people at the headquarters in California and generally making a nuisance of himself. I'm not sure what he was playing at, but at the heart of it would have been self-promotion and the opportunity to trash everyone around him. That was his style.

My worst personal experience of Simon (and there were many) was the aftermath of attending a management conference in Palm Springs. For some unknown reason, Rob had decreed that we should fly economy class, even though company policy allowed us to fly business class. I was a bit miffed, particularly as we were returning early on a Saturday morning and I had a wedding to attend in Bristol in the afternoon. The outbound flight was horrible, delayed and I was sat in between a group of noisy school children and drunk adults. Suffice to say I wasn't looking forward to travelling home in similar conditions. So, while in Palm Springs, I appealed to Rob to allow me to return business class and he agreed. When I got to the airport at LA, I upgraded my ticket at a cost of around $3,000. When I got back I claimed the money back in the normal way, through my business expense claim. Rob approved the claim and it was sent to accounts, but a couple of weeks later I still hadn't been reimbursed. I asked my PA to call and find out why. Apparently it had been blocked by the global head of HR with no reason being given. I called him to discover that Simon had raised a complaint, saying I wasn't a good team player and, even though I had the correct approvals, it wasn't reasonable to reimburse me. The HR bod agreed and so now I had not only upset a pretty important person but I was $3,000 out of pocket. I knew I had to work hard to recover my reputation with him. But I was really angry by his superior attitude and refusal to listen to my protestation. I had bought my house insurance through the company as it offered a good staff discount and surprisingly and coincidentally I lost my Rolex watch shortly after the incident and had to put in a claim, the amount for which, was almost exactly the same as the cost of the ticket that wasn't reimbursed. I was paid and heard nothing more on the matter.

I'm not entirely sure how it all ended with Simon and Avco, word had it that he sent a letter to the president of the global business essentially threatening physical violence if he wasn't promoted. Safe to say he was gone immediately after that news broke.

A replacement for Simon was found quickly. Colin McAllister, a 30-year veteran from Australia who was a stereotypical Australian. He was like a cross between Barney Rubble and Sir Les Patterson (the so-called Australian Cultural Attaché character of Barry Humphries). What you saw was exactly what you got and he was a rough and tumble, hard-hitting, roll your sleeves up, work hard play hard character.

I liked him, although he was another one who thought everything was all about the branches and screw everything else – nobody else had much value and they added nothing. In saying that, he knew that I had the support of Rob and also of the US headquarters, which made a big difference. Colin went along with most of what I was trying to do, although the price I had to pay was a big one. I was asked to plan and organise what seemed like almost continual 'recognition' trips, awards events and overseas meetings that allowed Colin to tour around Europe (and beyond) at the company's expense and playing golf at some of the best courses we could find. It was a hard life!

Quite early on in my Avco career (mid-1991) I had a message from someone in Australia, asking if I would interview one of their employees who was a UK national returning home and looking for a job in marketing. I did so and we ended up giving Karen a job working for Harty. We were still a very small department and did the normal social stuff and, by now, I regarded Harty, Phil and others as friends. They were able to act as such but still maintain the professionalism to operate effectively in their work. During an after-work social outing, I was chatting to Karen and I learned that she was a keen squash player, so I suggested we play. At the time there was no other motive but we played again and then we soon started seeing each other. Fast forward and it wasn't too long before she'd moved in with me. Previously, she was living with her brother and sister-in-law, which wasn't ideal for her. I had since moved into a nice rented apartment in a converted house in Windsor and Karen joined me there around Christmas 1991.

Motoring-wise, I reacquainted myself with the Renault GTA Turbo. Having sold my previous one in Hove, I purchased a later model in a very striking blue colour. It still really looked the business and never failed to give me a great driving experience. I sold it after about two years to a chap who worked for McLaren Racing in Woking and he told me the first thing he was going to do was get it chipped (hugely boosting the power). I remember thinking it was quite likely he would kill himself!

By 1992, work – and the Avco business – had turned a corner. Colin was generally behaving himself and I had agreement that our sales managers didn't need to bother trying to drum up business for the branches, who were less than useless when it came to managing relationships with retailers (the business needed retailers to sell finance agreements). Instead, we changed the focus to deal only with large regional or national retailers. It wasn't easy but we had some success and quickly realised that the branches were equally useless in turning around the increasing volumes of business in good time or with any consistency.

As a result, we established what we called the National Sales Centre to process all the business centrally. Initially, it was just a few staff tucked away in a corner of the office, but it was an ideal job for Phil to manage and develop for the future. I had plans for several hundred staff if we could develop a good sales pipeline. We had also bought a small business from TSB Bank that loaned money to trade union members at preferential rates and set up another small centralised unit in Basingstoke. It was at that site where I first met Stewie (Marshall) who had previously been in audit. He was transferred to me to run the fairly small, self-contained business unit.

Due to Colin hosting numerous and almost endless incentive trips every year, my golf was improving considerably and I also had the 'unpleasant' task of having to travel the world assessing potential venues for where Colin could go next. I recall feeling guilty – the company didn't make oodles of money but it was growing its profitability (although not in a sustainable way, but nobody seemed to care). As a consequence, Colin was able to justify spending large sums of money on recognition and rewards for his people, although the overriding motive was for him to get free holidays and boost the balances of his numerous frequent flyer accounts.

We worked hard on developing our sales approach (and because I hated sales), I got Andy Pickard across from Amex to run the function. With Harty, Phil, Andy, and Stewie in place, I most certainly had a great little team – and a vast improvement on what I found when I arrived. We started to push good volumes of sales through the business, which ended up in the branches who were then supposed to support our central marketing effort and convert those sales customers into direct loan customers. The whole strategy was perfect, except the branches were just hopeless at doing their bit. Oh well, we couldn't have done more.

We did so many hilarious trips that I could probably dedicate an entire book to those alone. For example, Costa Del Sol – one night we had dinner overlooking a small bullfighting ring. As part of the entertainment, they asked for two volunteers to have a go. They obviously didn't realise what a macho business we were. There was no shortage of volunteers and the organisers picked two of the district managers. They went into the ring and a small bull with tennis balls stuck on the end of its small horns emerged. Clearly well trained, it snorted and scratched its hoofs in an intimidating way and headed for the two brave men. Two minutes later, the bull was on its back, legs akimbo and with the host having to drag off the two assailants before the bull was killed!

Portugal - 50 people and their partners went on a five-day reward trip, which included lots of golf. I had asked Rob if we could give them £200 each as a bit of extra spending, which he didn't think was a great idea. I protested that they had quite a lot of free time and it would be a decent thing to do, but he wouldn't budge. So I got Woody (our agency contact) to increase the invoice by £10,000 and give it to me in cash at the airport. On the flight and in the hotel I distributed £200 (in local currency) to each of the attendees. Funnily enough, when we got back, Rob said to me: "See? We didn't need to give them any money, they all enjoyed themselves anyway."

Deauville - yet another trip that was heavily golf-centric. One evening we ended up in a delightful traditional fish restaurant along the quayside in Trouville. Someone on our table ordered fruits de mer and the biggest platter I've ever seen turned up. Dave Boss (lovely chap who sadly died on the day he was retiring) picked up a giant prawn and asked 'what do I do with this?' and someone replied "You pull the head off and eat it." So he pulled the head off and ate it (the head)!

The restaurant wasn't cheap and Colin and his crew were never backwards in coming forwards when it came to spending company money. The food and booze were flowing freely and Rob was loving the ambience and traditional nature of the venue and, as an unaccomplished drinker by company standards, was getting very tipsy. When the bill arrived, Rob insisted on giving the waiter a 15% tip which, if I recall came to about £300. The waiter was so appreciative that he went away and came back with four bottles of champagne for us. Rob was so thrilled he gave him another £100!

After dinner, four of the group wanted to go to the Casino across the road but needed a passport to get in. They didn't have one between them, but I did so I gave it to Phil or Harty and said they could try. Whoever got in first managed to find a window, passed out the passport to the second who got in, who then passed it to the third and finally the fourth. The management were suspicious from the off and got all four together and asked them for passports. Of course, only one was handed across. The manager looked at it, asked who Tony Cooper was and they all answered in unison, "I am!"

Adaire Manor - this is a wonderful southern Irish golf resort, which has since hosted the Irish Open. The course, designed by legendary golf course architect Robert Trent Jones, was brand new and not even open yet. We spent four nights in the hotel and, on the last night, having spent thousands in the bar and restaurant, we were all grouped together in the bar area. Colin announced that we needed to be out for 07.00 the following morning to get to the golf course two hours away, for a 09.00 tee off, before heading back to Cork for a 15.00 flight. The hotel manager overheard this and, being so happy that we had probably generated a whole month's revenue in four days, offered us the exclusive use of the course the following morning. He explained that it was all ready to go, ahead of a grand opening the following weekend. We were thrilled – an extra two hours in bed and the opportunity to play a superb championship course. We could even have a 'shotgun start' so the 32 players were sorted into groups of four and each picked a different tee to start from so we would all finish at the same time. Perfect!

The next day we duly arrived on the tee and hit our drives. When we got to our balls and ready to play the second shot into the green we were understandably disappointed to see that there was no flag in the green. No problem, we weren't professionals so just aim for the centre of the green. But when we got to the green, we discovered there weren't actually any holes cut. We briefly thought about putting a score card in the centre of the green and pretend that was the hole but quickly abandoned that idea. 20 minutes later we were back in the bar having a mid-morning beer or two.

Cyprus - Harty and I had already endured a pretty entertaining inspection trip to check out the hotel, where we were shown the Presidential suite that the Sultan of Brunei had spent over £1m decorating to his taste for a three-night stay. On the trip out one of the cabin crew asked Harty if he wanted to sit on the flight deck as we were coming into land (before the days of hijacking and bomb terrorism), which he gratefully accepted. When the seat belt sign went on to signify our approach Harty asked when he would be called up to the cockpit to which the lady replied 'the Captain has said that you shouldn't come up on account of the drinking'. Harty responded aghast by saying, 'drinking, the Captain has been drinking?!'

Cyprus was the annual all-manager conference – essentially just another excuse for golf, drinking and eating to excess. But one of the traditions of the conference was that we would have an after dinner speaker (comedian) on the final night. It was a tough audience, so the pressure was on me to find the right act. For the entire five days we had an overall budget of £300,000 but, as was the norm, Colin started adding stuff like T-shirts, golf balls and extra dinners or drinks receptions here and there. By the time I managed to rein him in we were left with less than half what I needed to get the right comedian. I went to Woody and he gave me a lot of very uninspiring names. In the end I very reluctantly agreed to go with Roger de Courcey, a ventriloquist who came with Nookie Bear. In the past the entertainers had been the likes of, Frank Carson, Mike Reid and that ilk, not my cup of tea.

I was petrified. If he wasn't a complete success both he and I would be dead meat. To make matters worse, our new head of HR (Dick Love, a bible-thumping Aussie who resembled a spitting image puppet) had come to me beforehand and said he had heard about these raucous events. He made it clear that he didn't want to hear any bad language or gags that were feminist, racist or attempted to poke fun at pretty well anyone. These guys were used to X rated acts and here was I under instruction to produce an act more suitable for 7 year olds! As was the tradition, the identity of the after dinner speaker was kept confidential and would only be revealed at dinner as they would sit next to me and would be recognised. I did contemplate coming up with some excuse to have to fly home to avoid the expected lynching but I couldn't come up with anything credible.

Roger De Courcey arrived in the hotel late afternoon and I had arranged to meet him in a quiet area for a beer and to brief him. I had Paul Soper with me who was in the Operations Management group and a really funny guy. We weren't then, but have since become good friends. Paul had actually delivered an after dinner cameo a year or two earlier as a 'warm up' for someone like Frank Carson and, whoever the comic was that followed, made a point that Paul was going to be a hugely tough act to follow. Anyhow when I told De Courcey that he wasn't to use bad language or tell any stories that might cause anyone any offence, he groaned and told me that I had just eliminated 90% of his act and that we should have booked the well known children's act, Sooty and Sweep. I was in a jam, I had little choice but to tell him to go ahead, "deliver your act and I'll live with the consequences." I needn't have feared – to this day he was one of the funniest comedians I have ever seen and he brought the house down. I don't think Dick Love dare protest, he would have been slaughtered.

In mid-1992, Karen and I moved to a rented house (I still hadn't sold my house in Hove at this point) just outside Woking and, in early 1993, she became pregnant with Fran. Thankfully I did eventually sell the house in Hove and we found a house to buy in Camberley (house owned number six), which we moved into when Fran was about three months old.

Francesca was born in September 1993 and introduced me to the pleasures of fatherhood. Even though I had plenty of time to think it through; like any new parent I was ill prepared. I loved it and it made me feel very different about myself. I was looking forward to all of the obvious milestones and experiencing the numerous phases of her life. I knew that work would be a potential obstacle but I thought I could cope with that.

In early 1994, out of the blue I had a phone call from Dave Fretter. I'd lost contact with him, for no other reason than I was busy with work and other things in my life. He was struggling – he had left HFC two or three years after me and set up his own kitchen and bathroom business, which hadn't been a success. He then had a couple of other jobs, but was fired from both of them. It tickled me that he liked to say that he'd been fired from every job he had ever had and it was 100% true! Dave was a bit of a loose canon and not everyone's cup of tea, but he was and is a very decent bloke. He asked if I could do anything to help him get a job. I duly got him an interview as a district manager at Avco working in Colin's team. I gave him a glowing reference and they hired him. I remember saying to Dave that this was a big deal for me (and it was) and that I had to work really hard on Colin, so Dave had to behave himself, as I knew he had the capability of not doing so.

Dave went off to run a few branches in the Midlands so

our paths didn't really cross. But, after only about four weeks, Rob Plumb called me into his office where I was confronted by him and Colin to be told that someone had reported Dave for inappropriate drunken behaviour at the end of his four-day induction programme (a residential programme they ran every month for all new employees) and he was now on a warning. I defended him as best I could and then called him when I left Rob's office to tell him to be very very careful. Less than three months later, I learned (I wasn't around at the time) that Dave had been tasked with entertaining suppliers at a Test Match at Lords. Unfortunately, he had been rude to some of the old boys in the MCC lounge and the company had received an official complaint about him. I'm sure it wasn't such a big deal, but he was always up against it. The operations side of the business were pretty Neanderthal and regarded themselves as something of a closed shop, so they didn't need much of a reason to get rid of him. He was fired on the spot and I was sorry about that as I am sure matters had been blown out of proportion but I couldn't get any more involved. I didn't hear from him again for several years.

I made my second trip to Amsterdam in 1994, the occasion being Harty's stag do. There were eight or nine of us and it was a riot. We had a hotel but I'm not sure we actually got to use it other than dump our bags and maybe grab an hour or two of sleep. We were all pretty well behaved, but made a bit of a beeline for the tea shops and I had my second experience of a spliff, but was much better prepared for it. It did tickle me to see grown men in fits of laughter over absolutely nothing. Phil didn't partake and was quickly labelled one of The Righteous Brothers. We spent the weekend doing what people do on stag dos: drinking; eating and smoking. We found a fabulous bar near the central station that played really good music and spent most of the time there. I've not been on a great many stag do's, but that stands out as the best.

In mid-1994, business was booming and I was invited to join a major project for up to eight months at the California head office. The plan was to lead a small team, under the guidance of a well known firm of consultants, I will refer to them as M&M, to develop a new business strategy. The whole global business (US, Canada, UK and Australia) was suffering the same issue: a diminishing customer base. The only way to keep profits increasing was to lend more and more money to the same people, which simply wasn't sustainable. I think those at the top recognised what I was trying to do in terms of reshaping our UK business and thought I would offer good input.

We had a fun time in California. We were housed in a nice, low rise apartment complex along with others who had been drafted in from around the world as well as other parts of the US. Given that I (we) pretty well knew the outcome before starting the six months of work meant that we treated the whole experience as a work-based holiday. I got to travel all over the world on the pretext of research and data-gathering and had a very generous expense allowance to allow me to do pretty well what I wanted. The project culminated in a major presentation we gave to the parent company management board in Providence, Rhode Island and at which they accepted all the recommendations. The plan required a complete transformation of the business at a cost of around $180m, which is a lot of money now, let along back in 1994! I never actually subscribed to the $180m number for two reasons: 1) it required the business to build a completely new IT system, which I didn't think necessary (buy one instead) and 2) out of the $180m there was approximately $70m of M&M costs and I didn't think we needed more than a fraction of that. Furthermore, M&M had front loaded its costs so that the vast majority was billed in the first 18 months. The cynic in me said that was to get all their money before anything went wrong, how right I was about that! But my work was done and there was no benefit in my 'rocking the boat'.

The most amusing thing about the whole affair was that this six-month period of research pulled in 10-12 full time employees from the business (and scores of part-timers), had at least six full-time M&M consultants plus support and cost the business somewhere in the region of $7m, ended up with a 70-page document that recommended precisely what we were doing in the UK. Typical consultants – no wonder people think they are people who would borrow your watch to tell you the time, keep the watch and then charge you for the privilege!

Rather than coming home for Christmas in 1994, Karen and I decided to go up to Lake Tahoe for a skiing trip. We also planned to get married while we were there and booked a really lovely little wooden church, not much bigger than a large garage, for the ceremony. Apart from the minister and Fran, the only other person there was a witness who, I think, was another staff member at the church. They were happier times of course and we had a wonderful time.

At work and having made a presentation at the conclusion of the project the team spent a few days tidying up loose ends and we returned to the UK and I went back into my old job and settled back into life at home, everything was as it was before. That was until about four months later, in June 1995, when the president of the business called me and said: "You told us what we needed to do and why, but you didn't tell us how, so I want you to come back over for four years and lead the initiative across the globe." There wasn't a great deal to think about: the financial package was outstanding and Karen and I were both excited at the prospect of living in southern California.

10 - MISSION VIEJO

I went ahead of Karen – as she was expecting Stephanie – and I lived in a Hyatt hotel for the first few months. Steph was born in October 1995 and, by then, I had found us a house to rent on a gated community in Mission Viejo, about 40 miles south of LA and 10 miles from work. Once Stephanie was born we rented out our house in Camberley and Karen and the girls moved over.

At any other time of day, the time to travel between home and work would have taken about 20 minutes. But the commuter traffic on the I-405 meant that, during rush hour, the journey was an hour, on a good day. I eventually settled into a routine of leaving home at 06.30 with an intention of leaving the office by 16.00, but that rarely happened.

I was given a team of business people from around

our global network and I was able to get Phil to come and work with me on a full-time basis, so he and Ceris moved over and rented a house two streets away. That helped enormously, just having someone there that I knew well and trusted.

One of my early recollections was going to get our cars. We went to the area in town where all the car dealers were lined up next to each other and, not only did we chose our cars there and then, we were even able to specify colour, trim and whatever extras we wanted because they had them all in stock. It was bizarre, we literally drove them off the same day, me in a sporty Nissan 300ZX, Karen in a Nissan 4x4 thingy.

Work was rewarding, in the sense that I had a huge responsibility, which was added to shortly after we started by being given responsibility for all the IT staff as well as the business side of things. On the other hand, the stress levels were enormous, not because of the responsibility, but because it became quickly apparent to me that the leadership team had been sold a pup, totally misled by very convincing M&M consultants.

Jumping a few years forward, the programme ultimately failed for two principal reasons. Firstly, the advice M&M gave was totally flawed – we should have purchased an off-the-shelf IT package and customised it, but that would have made it much harder to justify M&M's immense costs. Secondly, M&M massively overstated their expertise and the degree to which they could help us. At one point I think they had upwards of 60 consultants on the programme, billing us an average of $1,000 a day. I argued (to the point of committing career suicide) that more than 50 of them added zero value whatsoever and we didn't need them. Unfortunately the M&M engagement director was a wise old dog with form, and he had clearly planned for such push back. He had obviously spent many months brainwashing the senior management and covered all the bases. Also, M&M had solid relationships right through to the parent company, board and president. I was quite simply outgunned. Then, immediately after we kicked off the work of the program, the president of our business decided that each of our countries should pay the total cost from their profits for the next five years, <u>BUT</u> they still had to make the profit that they were expected to make without these costs being added. If ever I witnessed a potential rebellion in a company it was then. As the public face of the program I was put straight into the firing line and all the goodwill I needed from the individual country heads evaporated before my eyes. My task had just been made infinitely more challenging, perhaps impossible.

So the work was hard, probably the hardest of my life and much harder than it needed to be. It was probably the only time in my entire career that I had been truly stressed. But there were highlights, not least when I eventually convinced our senior management to change course – too late, but I got there. It saved the company some money but by then they were being gobbled up by another business, so all the good work we had done was ultimately lost anyway.

Living in California had its ups and downs. From a social perspective there was a lot of juggling to be done given that work consumed such a large amount of my waking time. But I joined the local golf club, a very high-quality (but far from the highest) facility with a $25,000 down payment and monthly fees of $500, a whole different world to home. I got in with a fairly large group of British ex-pats and Californian Anglophiles and because of the work hours I was doing I was able to carve out every Friday afternoon for golf, when not away travelling. That was about the extent of my social life. Oddly, for such an elite environment, I found the people there that I associated with to be by far the most down to earth of any.

Fran went to a nursery/playgroup most days and Karen settled in well exploring and chilling as best she could with a newborn baby. I tried to balance my life between work, the weekly game of golf and undertaking dad/husband duties, neither of which I was brilliant at. Like many couples with two young children there was a fair amount of stress present – and my job certainly didn't help – but we muddled through. I do remember though feeling utterly exhausted by the time the weekends arrived and that wasn't good for Karen and the girls who had been waiting for me to do all the weekend things.

We had a shock when Steph was just under a year old when she had a seizure. We didn't know what was happening or what to do, but we ended up in hospital and they decided to give her a lumbar puncture to check for meningitis. We watched and it was the most frightening experience. I remember Steph looking at us with an expression that asked: "Why on earth are you letting them do this to me?" I was heartbroken. As a child of similar age I had also suffered seizures so I assumed it to be hereditary. She had three more seizures over the next year and each time was as scary as the last. Her temperature would rocket up to 40 degrees and more in a matter of minutes and the only remedy was to immerse her body in a bath of cold water, which itself warmed up with her body heat, so it needed up to three refills before she stabilised. We were told she would grow out of it and, thankfully she did.

Work was becoming increasingly difficult, I could see M&M draining money from us and we were getting minimal value, nothing much to show for it, but I was still having great difficulty convincing our management board to change course. I think this was due to them selling the whole programme and benefits to the parent company board to secure the investment. Now that several million dollars had been spent, there was a reluctance to announce anything other than good news. Even at those levels, I guess people were fearful of losing their job, as indeed some should have. On top of that, I was constantly travelling the world trying to keep country leadership teams onside and supportive – extremely difficult when I didn't believe in what we were doing myself! It was an impossible situation, I was fielding all sorts of questions that not only did I not have the answers to, but I wanted answered myself. I became a master of thinking on my feet. Finally, I made a breakthrough with my boss – the vice chairman – and he agreed, initially privately, that we should change course. I then needed to travel all over the US, talking to tech businesses and software integrators to find a better and more affordable solution. But, throughout this time, M&M were still billing us several million dollars a month for something that I knew was going to be thrown away.

Travel was such a big part of my working life and it had its ups and downs – literally! One notable trip I made was to London, Ontario. It was the headquarters of the Canadian business and I visited frequently because the president there was the most influential of all the country presidents. I knew if I could get him onside, my job would become infinitely easier. To get to London I had to take a direct flight from Orange County to Detroit (four hours) and then switch to a small 'puddle-jumper' for the 40-minute flight to London. I am a terrible flyer at the best of times but these little aircraft that resembled Airfix models were the most frightening.

On this occasion, it was the depths of winter and we landed in Detroit in driving snow and I was convinced the short flight to London would be late or cancelled, but at the gate they were happily boarding. The plane had eight rows and just two seats a row. When I boarded I noticed the plane was extremely brightly lit and hot! I sat down and the seat in front was occupied by a very tall man and, I noticed that his head was actually touching the single light above. Not long after that, I saw his hair begin to smoke, from the intense heat of the very bright light. Before I could warn him that he appeared to be catching fire, he realised what was happening, moved his head aside and then stuffed tissue paper over the light. I was about to have a heart attack, fearing that we were all about to go up in smoke but that fear was soon dispelled when there was a loud bang and all the lights went out! Emergency lighting came on and the captain announced that, due to an electrical fault, there would only be low level lighting for the duration of the flight. I was delighted!

I still didn't think we would be taking off due to the snow but, shortly after, we pushed back and set off down the runway. The take-off was as if a paper plane had been put into a wind tunnel, the strangest of feelings and we were thrown around like crazy but, somehow, we got above the low cloud and things calmed down a little. But oddly, about every 30-45 seconds there was a clunk from the left side wing (which was on top of the aircraft) and a noticeable lurch sideways. My fears were soon heightened yet another notch (well several notches) when the pilot announced that he was unable to retract the landing gear on the left side (which hangs down beneath the wing) and that our arrival may be delayed by 10 minutes or so. He said he would keep trying to retract the gear and, if successful, we could make time up. There was one flight attendant on board and I didn't hesitate to ask her to tell the captain that I was more than happy being 10-15 minutes late and just leave the damn wheels down! Fortunately, he wasn't successful and we landed late, but alive! I made several trips to London, Ontario after that but never used that route again, instead opting to hire a hire car in Detroit and drive the 100 miles or so into Canada.

Talking of flights, I often had to fly within the US and our local airport (John Wayne, Orange County) was very convenient and a very good alternative to the horrid LAX. The airport had opened about 4 or 5 years earlier amid much controversy, which I was unaware of. On my first flight we were taxiing out to the runway, the normal safety announcements had been made and then the captain came on and added his greetings. But he also said that if anyone hadn't flown from this airport before then the departure was a little different but not to be concerned. I recall vividly wanting to get off right there and then!

All flights there take off to the west as the prevailing winds are west to east. So flights take off in the direction of the beaches about four miles away, with some of the most expensive real estate in the world. Seemingly at the time that planning permission was being sought, the very influential owners of these properties objected and a difficult compromise was struck after years of impasse.

Anyway our plane (a Boeing 757) was at the end of the runway and the engines fired up and power increased so much that the plane was violently shaking, so much that I expected the windows to fall out! The pilot didn't release the brakes until it felt like we were at maximum power, and when he did we were catapulted down the runway. Within seconds we were airborne with the engines still running at full power but it felt like we were heading almost straight up as if in a rocket launched from Cape Kennedy to the moon! The noise was deafening and the vibration terrifying, there was no let up. Then, all of a sudden, at about 5,000ft there was total silence. I was convinced the engines had simply blown themselves off the aircraft. The nose came down and from heading almost straight up, we were now in a pretty steep descent and everything went very very quiet and very very still. I'm checking the reaction of the other passengers, most look fine, some even asleep, it didn't help. I saw the coastline ahead and remember thinking we could probably ditch in the sea and I might just survive this. We must have got about a mile out to sea and were now down to something like 2,000ft when the engines came to life in a far more controlled fashion and we began a steady climb and were on our way. I learnt afterwards that permission to build the airport was only given once the airport authority agreed a plan that the noise of the aircraft would not intrude upon the peace of the mega rich property owners, hence the planes gliding out over the coastline. After that, I rarely used Orange County preferring to take my chances on the zoo that is LAX.

I can't mention trips without recalling a journey we made to Australia. I don't remember when it was but we flew LA-London-Sydney-LA. We needed to go down there, run a couple of fact-finding and information gathering workshops with large groups of business people to help us with a specific bit of build and we needed to run a couple of similar events in the UK. After we had completed our UK leg, Phil and I were joined by Martin, a UK-based mid level manager. The UK programme leader had decided it would be useful for him to join us and understand what was being done elsewhere.

We flew down there in Club and arranged it so that we had a 36 hour lay over in Bangkok. After we boarded at Heathrow for the overnight flight, Phil suggested we play cards (in those days the middle seats in Club were three abreast) and he suggested nine-card brag. Martin wasn't too happy because "you can play it for hours and nobody ends up winning anything". As it was, Martin got off the flight 12 hours later having lost the best part of £600. Although an overnight flight, we were intent on staying awake and played cards throughout. The rest of the cabin was in darkness apart from one seat towards the rear occupied by Simon Ward, a well-known actor who shot to fame for his role in the film Young Winston. He stayed awake throughout the entire flight drinking and laughing with his companion which impressed Phil so much that we decided he would be the winner of our (just then) created Simon Ward award.

I had been to Bangkok before and I had briefed the other two. We would go to our hotel (Phil and Martin had to share a room, but I had my own), shower, change and meet in the lobby half an hour later for a shopping trip. That all went like clockwork and we met as planned, although I wasn't sure about Martin wearing his replica Leeds shirt and shorts, along with brown ankle socks and Hush Puppies – but each to their own. We hailed a three seater Tuk-Tuk and I told the driver via attempted sign language (he spoke no English) to take us to where we could get Rolex watches, Lacoste shirts and Gucci handbags. We shot off, coming close to death on several occasions on the ridiculously overcrowded roads filled with suicide-seeking drivers. After a short journey we arrived outside a four storey building of market-type stalls and the driver took us inside to one particular stall. But, it was just full of bric a brac and novelty stuff, so I told him "No, we want Rolex watches, Lacoste T-shirts and Gucci handbags!" He nodded and enthusiastically made noises suggesting he understood, so we got back on the Tuk-Tuk and sped off through the jam-packed streets. We arrived outside a tailors and he gestured us in. I told him that this didn't look like what we wanted, but he was insistent. Stupidly, we went in and all three of us were pretty well leapt on by over-enthusiastic tailors who wanted to measure us up for "Wery good suits, weady tomorrow". We managed to escape the shop and, this time, I was more insistent with our driver – to the point of threatening assault if he didn't take us to where we could get Rolex watches, Lacoste shirts and Gucci handbags. After several minutes of very difficult 'conversation' it turned out that he was getting vouchers from the establishments he was taking us to, which he exchanged for petrol. I gave him the equivalent of about £5 and 10 minutes later we were in the heart of a huge area selling everything we needed and more.

We got back to the hotel, dropped the shopping off and I told Phil and Martin I would introduce them to the delights of Patpong. I don't know what it's like today, but 30 or so years ago it was wild. We wandered down the main street and although it was the quietest time of the day, we were approached several times to go into this bar or that bar where all sorts of delights were waiting for us. But, having done one complete circuit, we decided to stop at a fairly innocuous-looking bar, which had a completely open frontage, that made us feel safe! The bar serving area was in the centre and the bar top was a big square around the outside. It was fairly quiet and we picked three seats at the bar and ordered our beers. Within minutes we were surrounded by half a dozen girls and it was all really quite unpleasant. We made our distaste very clear and they eventually got the message and left us alone.

On the opposite side of the bar were two men – they looked like tourists – and one was gesturing us over. I went across, they were Scottish and they were either residents or regular visitors. One of them said: "You might want to be careful here, they are all boys" I went back to the other two and told them what had been said and we all stared very intently at the 'girls' who had now retreated to an area behind us, none of us could tell at all that they weren't, really quite attractive, girls. It was a very strange experience indeed.

After returning to our hotel for an afternoon nap we met in the lobby and headed off to a very nice restaurant which had been recommended and then decided to stop off at Patpong on the way back to see what it's like at 10.00 at night. It was absolutely buzzing and we picked a random bar and went in. Apart from the customers, there must have been 70-100 Thai girls circulating and all had numbers on a band on their wrists. We learnt that this was because they could be ordered by simply giving the number to the bartender, I certainly hope that sort of thing doesn't still go on, it was exploitation on an industrial scale. We drank our beer up quickly but, as we went to leave, Martin hooked up with a young Thai girl whose name appeared to be 74. I asked him what he was doing and he said he wanted to take her back to the hotel. Phil objected, not least because they were sharing a room and I simply 'ordered' him to leave her there, she wasn't getting in any tuk tuk with us! As it happened nor did Martin!

We got to Sydney the next day and prepared for four days of meetings and workshops. On the first evening, Martin came to me and announced that he had come out in a rash and asked if he could be excused the next morning so he could seek medical help. Thankfully, he had acquired nothing more than some kind of minor infection??? The rest of the trip passed off without too much drama, but it was one that lived long in the memory, for all sorts of reasons!

Back in the US, we often had big workshops with a constant coming and going of people from around the world in large numbers, which took a lot of organising. One time when focussing on Australian requirements seven of them showed up for about 10 days. They were stereotypical Australians (Boguns, as Stephanie calls them) with a work hard; play hard mentality. This group told me they wanted to go to Vegas for the weekend and did I know where they should stay and how to get there? Now, I loved Vegas but had to ration my visits there for good reason - Karen would allow me to go once every three months or so, but any more would have been unreasonable and cause issues. I told them I could book them a hotel (I had preferential rates at Treasure Island) and would rent a van and drive them over.

On the Friday afternoon, we joined the exodus on the I-15 and arrived in Vegas around 5.00 and checked in. I suggested we all meet in reception about 20 minutes later when my plan was to take them to Caesers, play the tables for an hour or so and then head to the Bellagio for dinner. We met in reception as agreed and they immediately said they wanted to go to a strip club. To say I was disappointed would have been an understatement, but I thought 'OK, let's get this over with and we can still be back in the Bellagio for dinner at 8.00pm and then kick on from there'. I didn't know anything about strip clubs and so I asked the concierge, who gave me names of a few to try. They were all a drive away and off the Strip. We picked one at random and headed off. I can honestly say I do not find such establishments in any way entertaining, but I went in with the Aussies and headed for the bar while they all sat down and waited for their 'table service'. It was all pretty harmless, I suppose – half dressed young ladies smiling, serving their drinks and sitting on their laps while the Aussies slipped dollar bills into the sides of their briefs, wristbands or anywhere they could get them. After about 45 minutes, I suggested we should move on and thankfully they agreed. We went back to the van but, instead of agreeing to go to The Wynn or Venetian, they wanted to go to another strip club. After some heated debate we went. It was just like the first place, but they spent another hour there. They then wanted to go to another and it was at this point I gave them the list of establishments that the concierge gave me and left them to it. In fact, they spent the entire weekend in strip clubs, whereas I spent most of it either ferrying them around or on my own at one of the large hotels. Not the most enjoyable Vegas weekend for me, but I guess they had fun!

Work life in California continued to be tough but I tried to do my bit at home. Karen had acquired a season ticket for Disney World, which wasn't my cup of tea but

I was dutiful – well, sometimes. We spent time at the beach and doing the stuff that young families do (Sea World, San Diego Zoo, Universal Studios and general outdoors things) but it was never enough and I knew I was challenged between work, my own (much needed) downtime and family responsibilities. It caused tension and there simply weren't enough hours in the day. The pressures of work were also telling and I realised, probably for the first time, that I had a whole lot of emotional baggage as a result of my childhood. Karen found a counsellor and I agreed to go with her to see him but, even at the first session, he launched into me with both barrels, I was so totally unprepared. I was horrified at the end of the session to hear him announce that he didn't think that Karen and I had a future together. I assumed he would try and help us (me/her) resolve the problems, work on the deficiencies but he didn't seem too interested, It was a bizarre experience. I remember thinking I could really use his help but just not getting any. I guess one of the reasons was that I was still unable to properly open up and that would have limited his capability to get to the bottom of things. Although we soldiered on for a while, It was after that first meeting that I think we both knew we were doomed as a married couple.

By now the work programme was essentially suspended and the business was being sold to a competitor (The Associates, later to be acquired by Citibank) and it was difficult to see how any programme would continue. The sale of the business completed and I was offered a pretty big job at its HQ in Dallas. What with our marriage issues, the thought of heading to Texas in a brand new job was daunting, but I was pressured by the business and so I flew over for a few days to take a look around. I recall lots of bugs – many of them flying, most crawling, open backed trucks with huge wheels and shotguns visible in the back of the cab and it seemed as if the entire population wore cowboy boots, blue denim jeans and cowboy hats. Fish out of water sprang to mind. But, on the plus side, property was a fraction of the price of California and, as the job offer was permanent, I went to look at houses. The best being one came with two swimming pools (one indoors) and a three-hole golf course! All for the price of our relatively small four-bed house in Camberley.

But it wasn't going to be enough to save the marriage and nor did I feel at all comfortable about Dallas or, indeed, the company or the job. My boss was brilliant and agreed a fairly decent severance deal and also shipped all of our stuff back to the UK. It was the end of an era – in many aspects a great few years – but it also signalled the end of my second marriage. I probably paid the high price for having to commit so much time to my work, but separating was the best option, for sure. It also meant the end of my role as a live in Dad, which was undoubtedly the biggest regret of my entire life and caused me the most extreme and endless sadness.

11 - ROLLER COASTER

When we returned to the UK in early 1998, Karen and the girls went in one direction and I went in the other. Although she and I had ongoing 'niggles' around money, the financial settlement surrounding our divorce was agreed pretty quickly. I was determined that my girls would not have to go short as a consequence of the separation and I believe I was more than fair in every respect. We planned out things well in advance. Karen moved into a new-build house between Portsmouth and Southampton and the children were quickly settled into school.

I had a good working relationship with a leading headhunter in London and, prior to coming back, I had interviewed by phone, by video and also in person, successfully securing myself a job with a recently de-mutualised building society, The Woolwich, as director of retail savings. The job was based up at its head office in Bexleyheath – or so I thought, because when I arrived on day one my boss told me that my office was the former chairman's office at the old headquarters in Woolwich. It was only about six miles away, towards central London, but in a fairly run down area and the offices were very 1920s, in every respect.

For those of you familiar with the TV programme 'Are You Being Served?', the business reminded me of that – a throwback in every respect. The building, the people and the culture – which came across as 'don't work too hard, don't invest any money and don't worry too much about growing the business'. For someone who had worked all their life for hard-nosed, dynamic and almost ruthless US businesses, it was a shock of gargantuan proportions. My office, about 15' square, had a big oak desk and proper leather chair (with no wheels) and another desk that had draws for paper and envelopes, but nothing functional. My name was on the outside of a big oak door that had a huge spring mechanism that kept it closed. The only window was behind me – it could be opened but I soon discovered not to do so because pigeons would fly in! Once in my office I was completely cut off from the outside world. On the other side of my large oak door sat my secretary (PA). I'm ashamed to say, I don't remember her name, but she was a mature lady with 40 years' service and made nice cups of tea. I couldn't keep the door of my office open as even the strongest weight behind it was no match for the gigantic spring mechanism, so I spent much of my time either in solitary confinement or driving backwards and forwards between Woolwich and Bexleyheath for meetings, most of which were unnecessary. After three weeks, I asked my PA about the office next door to me that had the name Frank Bartlett on it and why I hadn't actually come across Frank. "Frank's retiring in a couple of years," she replied. "So he doesn't come in much any more." I think that one answer summed up the place perfectly.

I set up home in Chislehurst (a suburb of South East London) and purchased house number seven, quickly settling in. It was a drag down to where Karen lived to pick up and drop off the girls every other weekend, but I did it religiously. Shortly after Karen offered to meet me at Basingstoke services on the M3, thus cutting a good 30 miles each way off my journey. It didn't occur to me at the time, but it must have been tough on the girls, too, but they never once complained or tried not to come. I am so grateful for that and we muddled through our weekends OK, on the whole.

There was so much to do at work, The Woolwich was 20 years behind in every respect, but it was one of those legacy businesses ("We bank with The Woolwich because my Mum and Dad did") where no matter how badly you treated the customer, or how poor the products and services were, the customer remained loyal. But it was clear to see that the world was changing and a new breed of bank would be emerging that would wipe places like The Woolwich from the landscape if it didn't change. My team were all dyed in the wool Woolwich lifers and so I quickly called Harty and asked him to come and help. He was going to be more patient than I and probably do a better job in getting across the need for change – better than my "It's staring you in the face, you idiot!" approach.

Harty did indeed join me and we set about the herculean task of trying to change an entire organisation (at the time it was the sixth largest UK bank) with over 150 years of history almost single-handedly. I was no more than seven months into the job when the rumours started about a potential takeover by Barclays. It quickly dawned on me that one of the reasons I wasn't getting the investment funding I needed – and indeed being told to cut costs everywhere, regardless of the impact – was that the board was doing whatever it could to increase short-term profits, to drive up the ultimate selling price. As much as it might seem unrealistic, selling prices of these large publicly traded businesses normally do start out – and end up – in a range not far away from the established industry Price/Earnings ratio.

When I joined the Woolwich I negotiated an extra long notice period (one year) for the first 12 months just in case it was taken over (which many of their ilk were), therefore offering me some protection. But my contract also allowed me to serve the same one-year notice and, after less than nine months I knew I was going to leave, I hated the pedestrian nature of the business and general lack of commercial 'savvy'

My personal life was pretty non existent, I wasn't playing golf and so it was about having the children every other weekend and seeing friends in between. Karen was increasingly sociable and helpful. Once she said she would be happy to drive all the way up and drop the girls (I suspect she might have been curious to see where I lived), which she did and then did so a few times more until, eventually one weekend she just stayed over.

We became closer and during one conversation she asked if I was glad we had returned from California. That was easy, I most certainly wasn't. My marriage had broken down, I wasn't around to see my girls growing up and my job was, just, bizarre. She suggested that perhaps I go back, get another job (we now had the very much sought after green card; permanent residency) and then she and the girls would follow – and we would live happily ever after (my words not hers). I'm not sure how much thought I gave to it but I recall being very positive and shortly afterwards, I quit my job and put the house on the market.

I actually quit the Woolwich one day before my contract reverted to three months' notice from 12 months, which didn't make me popular at all. As is often the case at this level, they didn't want me to work my notice and so I was paid off in full. I knew Harty would be OK, he was far more adept than me at managing the obstacles and I left him in a good position and with a good reputation. The house in Chislehurst sold quickly, the furniture put into storage and, in mid-1999 I was on my way back to California to set up a new life.

I'd made several good friends in my time there and I asked Randy (and Susanne) if I could stay with them. He was one of the M&M consultants I had worked with, very capable and sympathetic to my cause and we would often talk and agree that we (Avco) were being misled by M&M management. He didn't last at M&M very long!

The problem with California from a work perspective was that there was very little in the way of financial services based there. This was largely due to the conservative banking laws that existed in the State, which made operating there unattractive. So, once I started to see the fruits of my networking effort I was being offered interviews in such places as New York, Chicago, Pittsburgh and Seattle – none of which I had any interest in living. I was happy to consider Arizona, Nevada, Georgia or Florida (and some of Texas) but beyond that I declined most of the approaches I received. So determined was I to achieve success that I told Karen that I wouldn't come home until I had been successful, it would drive me on. After three months, I was missing them all so much, video calls were no substitute.

I did finally get an approach for something that sounded OK. It was COO of a business that took over lottery wins and was based in Boca Raton, Florida. In those days, each of the 52 states ran its own lottery twice a week and so there were several hundred big winners each week. There was no opportunity to be anonymous and therefore twice a week this company, with a pretty slick telemarketing team, would contact all the big winners. At that time a US lottery win was not paid out in one go, but instead spread over 20 years. So a $3m winner would get $150,000 annually. The pitch was that the business could pay (let's say) $2m right now and the client assigns the win to the company. They can then really go and enjoy their winnings, rather than it being dripped to them over the years. OK, it didn't sound great but they were a very profitable business, Boca Raton met the criteria and I was getting impatient! So I flew over to Fort Lauderdale and, even today, I can remember walking down the steps from the aircraft, onto the tarmac and feeling the most intense heat and humidity. I was wearing a suit and by the time I got into the terminal I was drenched. I think I decided there and then that this job would need to be exceptional to get me to put up with this weather for up to four months of the year.

I was interviewed by the CEO and VP of HR, both ex-American Express but I hadn't come across either of them. The interview was pretty straightforward until I asked how they were going to expand their business model – in other words, how they planned to grow. They took great pleasure in telling me that they had recently moved into workers' compensation payments. For instance, if a factory worker loses a limb at work in an accident and is awarded a payment of $50,000 a year for the rest of their life, this company would offer them a one-time cash payment in return for them assigning their compensation payment. I'd be surprised if by now I was able to hide my discomfort. But that was not all, the company was soon to launch a product for the terminally ill. If diagnosed with a terminal illness – and had life insurance – the company would make a one-time cash payment now "so you could enjoy what's left of your life". Like the other products, the deal was dependent on the client assigning the company as the beneficiary of their insurance. I can't remember my exact reaction, suffice to say I was horrified. One last thing they mentioned was that one of the functions reporting to this job was telemarketing and, given that some of the people in that department were making well in excess of $1m a year, how would I feel about that when my salary was only $200,000? I probably uttered something nonsensical. A few days later the headhunter called me with the good news that I was to be offered the job …. I declined!

I continued my search and had a few near misses, but eventually had a really interesting call from a headhunter looking for a COO for a bank called First National Bank of Marin. Marin is the area to the North of San Francisco and I flew up there to be interviewed. The administrative headquarters were there but the operating centre – where all the servicing, fulfilment, IT, marketing and product management was handled – was in Las Vegas. The first interview was a success and I was then called across to Las Vegas to meet the team there. It all went so well that I anticipated a job offer and I spent an extra couple of days in Vegas finding my way around (in places off the strip and downtown) and looking at a few houses. Property was very affordable and, for the budget that I had assigned, we could have got ourselves a real mansion.

I went back to California to wait for what I hoped would be a positive call. By now I was staying with Eric, who had also worked on the programme at Avco. Randy and Susanne were expecting their first child and it seemed reasonable to give them space - but the three months I spent there really helped and they kept me sane. I got the call about a week later and was offered the job and, on the call, we discussed terms and start dates, etc. I was thrilled. As soon as I put the phone down I called Karen to tell her the good news - I wasn't even remotely ready for the response I received, which was that she was now settling into life in the UK and no longer wished to return to the US. I don't recall how I reacted - shock, anger, shaken to the core, maybe? I waited until the next day and called Karen again just to make sure I had fully understood and that I could not persuade her, but she wasn't for turning. I quickly concluded that it was for the best and that talk of our reconciliation was fanciful. I called the headhunter to retract my acceptance and made plans to return home. I didn't hang around because there was nothing for me to stay for and I desperately missed the girls.

The sale of my house in Chislehurst had long completed and, with nowhere to go, Karen allowed me to stay with her. There was a half-hearted attempt at reconciliation while I was there, but it was never going to happen. Indeed, my only desire was to move out just as soon as possible. But that was complicated by the fact that I had no job and didn't know where I might end up living. I was having to start my life all over again.

12 - EnCard

The period between 1999 and 2001 might have been very short, in terms of my working life, but it was, without question, the most exciting and impactful period of my 40 or so years of work. To say I have experienced highs and lows in the workplace would be an understatement and, even today, I can say those 18 or so months had it all. I suspect there are few people who have had such an opportunity, can have felt the immense pride of accomplishment or the intense distress of losing something that they had worked so hard over. Despite the fact that the end result was not positive I wouldn't trade this period of my life for anything, it was the most incredible experience.

After all the activity I had been through in California over the previous five or six months, my phone rang frequently with opportunities within the US, all of which I rejected as I couldn't consider being away from my children. But then I get a call about an opportunity to join EnCard, a fairly new internet only credit card issuer based in San Francisco and whose business was growing rapidly. I had read and heard a lot about it and it was indeed mightily impressive, but I explained that I could not consider anything as I was now back in the UK on a permanent basis. To my delight the headhunter said EnCard were looking for someone to fill the position of CEO of the UK business, which it was yet to establish, but had recently been given approval to launch by its investment committee as well as the UK regulator.

I went through a couple of phone interviews before flying over to San Francisco, spending two days meeting all the senior people and the person who would be my boss: Brian Ragnick, one of the original investors. The offices were on Market Street downtown and everything about the place seemed totally different to what I had ever experienced. It reflected what it was: an internet only business but bear in mind the internet was still in its infancy. But, even in those 'pioneering' days, it operated and behaved so very differently. Lots of fun in the office, meals brought in every Friday and a very casual feel to the whole thing. Very little command and control, lots of inclusivity. This disguised and likely encouraged a tremendous work ethic, which could almost be touched.

It was so highly impressive, yet difficult to articulate precisely.

I was offered the role at the end of the second day of interviews and accepted it without hesitation, I couldn't wait to get stuck in. The product was both ground breaking and outstandingly advanced, compared with other cards on the market. Also, the people gave off an immense sense of enthusiasm, I could feel the excitement. If any business was ahead of the curve (and in mainstream banking there really aren't any) then this was it. I was offered a very good salary but the big carrot was the 500,000 share options I would be given and that I could purchase for $0.01 each after a three-year vesting period. On the day they made that offer they were trading then at a little over $20 and rising fast. At one point about a year later they peaked at around $40. It doesn't take much to realise that 500,000 x $40 is a very attractive incentive indeed.

After accepting the job I stayed for a further 10 days to talk to as many people as I could and get to really understand the business, its competitive advantages and what could and couldn't be lifted and shifted to the UK. It was a huge task but I was promised all sorts of subject matter expertise and functional help to support me as I built the business from the ground up. I certainly needed it – there weren't even any offices and my first job was to find one (where?) that could accommodate (how many?) the staff.

I arrived back 'home' with a work laptop, business

credit card, bank cheque book, rafts of papers describing the processes the US business went through to launch and a bunch of phone numbers and email addresses. About the only objective I had was to get a card business built from the ground up and taken through all the complex legal rigour and ready for launch by March 2001. I wasn't even given a budget – the business was awash with cash and I was simply told that my spending would be monitored and just be sensible! A bank account had been opened with Barclays and $2-3M deposited to start me off. I had about 17 months to be ready for launch, there was an enormous amount to do and I couldn't waste a second.

I still had no home and given that I had flown out to California for an interview and flown back with a huge, time pressing job I pretty well bought the first house that was available and I could move into immediately. So, house number eight, in Le Marchant Road, Camberley was purchased and occupied in literally days. It was handy for the mainline trains from Farnborough into Waterloo. I might not have had a work base at the time but I knew it would be central London, so Camberley worked well for that, plus I was familiar with it and it was fairly convenient for me to pick up and drop off the girls every other weekend.

I also treated myself to a new car, a rare and sought after Honda NSX. It was the car that Ayrton Senna used as his personal plaything and it was a real beauty – dark purple/blue and immensely powerful, the engine designed around the Honda F1 product.

Back at work, I managed to find serviced offices without a long lease with a perfect address: 100 Pall Mall - just down from Piccadilly Circus and sandwiched between The RAC Club and Institute of Directors. I signed a deal for office space for about 70 people and on (my) day one I arrived, picked my desk (it was all open plan of course) opened my laptop and started to wonder where to start. I had been making plans like crazy but suddenly, sat here, I was overcome by a huge - but thankfully short-lived - sense of fear. It was a most uncomfortable feeling.

At about 10.00 a young lady came in and asked "Are you EnCard?" I told her we (I) was and she gave me a letter from the landlords, welcoming the business, etc. She asked me what the business was all about and I gave her a brief account (I was grateful to have someone to talk to). It turned out that she was a temp working in reception on the ground floor and it was her first day, but she didn't like it as she was expecting something with a bit more responsibility. We chatted and I thought she was nice and sounded capable, so I offered her a job as my PA, there and then. She accepted immediately, went downstairs, quit and an hour later was sat at the desk next to me, just chatting. I hadn't anything for her to do but I appreciated the company! Welcome Heidi, employee number two.

I snapped out of my shock after a couple of days and set about my task with everything I could throw at it. I had notified my boss about the offices and 20 laptops showed up, all configured and ready to go. Thankfully I had been given a CIO (a very genial Irishman, Brendan) who had been working on the development in the US and he arrived a day or two later, so now it was Brendan, Heidi and me. I had made contact and met with Visa, the card scheme we would be using and the people there were very helpful in building out our plans. I also spoke with the Bank of Ireland (BoI), whose licence we were 'passporting' until our banking licence was approved, likely up to two years' later. Both Visa and BoI provided much-needed regulatory oversight and project resource.

Brendan really hit the ground running but he was 100% technical and he commandeered the largest meeting room we had and claimed it as his server room (so I just rented another couple of meeting rooms). He also, very quickly, started to draw up a very long list of equipment he needed along with some very scary costs.

I called Harty, desperate for the sort of help he could provide. I was confident I could do this but I needed someone to take a big chunk off my hands while I got everything up and running. I never blamed him for turning me down, he was settled in at The Woolwich, which had now been taken over by Barclays, had a young family and wasn't comfortable with taking on a new venture. I scoured my brain for an alternative and I came up with Eileen McMillan.

I worked with Eileen at Avco - she had the office next to me and was the financial controller. The (almost unique) thing about Eileen was she knew everything about every aspect of the business. She was one of those people who you could ask for a view on anything and she would have a good one. The breadth of her knowledge was incredible. On top of that, she was one of the most efficient and productive people I had ever come across. Quite how I don't know because her office was a total mess and it always looked as if it had been ransacked. She was always a mess and I don't think I ever saw her wearing makeup, I'm not sure she ever brushed her hair and most of the time her clothes were covered in food, either hers or that of her two young boys. Some years later she had applied for a big job at Lloyds bank and the recruiter called me asking for my views on her suitability. I told him if he interviewed 100 people she might well come last in his list. But, if he were to give all 100 the job she would undoubtedly outperform all the others and be the best. I can say, without fear of contradiction, that she was one of the most impressive people I ever worked with. She was a truly lovely person too, a great Mum and there was nothing about her you couldn't like, she had a huge heart. A big regret of mine – and something I have never really forgiven myself for – was that she developed a brain tumour a few years later and she called me when she knew she didn't have long to go. I dithered and didn't go over promptly to see her and by the time I planned to do so she had gone. I was – and still am – ashamed of myself for that.

Eileen had been with Avco for many years and I wasn't too optimistic about my chances of getting her to leave but, surprisingly, she did and she joined me after a few weeks and became my CFO. She also took on all of the legal and regulatory stuff (of which there were mountains of) and worked with our external lawyers as well as Visa and the Bank of Ireland. I validated just about everything with her – if Eileen was in agreement, I knew I wasn't going to be too wrong. We recruited like it was going out of fashion, I brought in John Hosie to run sales and marketing and Chris Fisher who worked with me at HFC and Amex to run operations. I had already earmarked the Bracknell/Reading corridor as the location for our operations centre – there was a lot of development there and a good labour pool. Brendan was busy recruiting all the technical people and we were so lucky to get hold of Nathan McIntyre, an outstanding developer who was an advanced programmer in the technologies we were using. Most of it was ground breaking, so finding experienced people was tough – and very expensive. We used iterative development and we could quite literally see the business building in front of our eyes. Within just three months, we had 70/80 people and the place was buzzing.

This is an example of the level of control we received from the US. Eileen would call her counterpart in San Francisco at the end of each month and simply tell him how much money we needed for the following month as we obviously didn't have any revenues. It was generally somewhere between £3 and £5m and it would be in our account almost instantly. If I knew then what I know now I might have been tempted to make it £6 or £7m for a month or two, they wouldn't have missed it!

I would talk to my boss three or four times a week by phone and and then join the company management meeting by video every Monday afternoon and update them. The resources I was promised never materialised as the US business was growing like wildfire, but it didn't bother me, I enjoyed the independence. After a few months I was totally on top of things and happy to plough on unhindered. One irritation, though, was a lady by the name of Haufin Tang. Haufin led the risk function in San Francisco, was very influential and wanted me to adopt the US credit risk rules almost entirely. I had managed risk at Amex and knew well that the US and UK markets behaved very differently, but she was not for moving and I feared that adopting the US rules would lead to issues downstream. Once I really dug into the US rules – as I needed to in order to build my case – I was not at all confident that they were well thought through. Indeed, I thought they had holes everywhere. Ultimately that was going to be so highly significant.

We had visitors: Haufin; IT people; product people; finance and legal people and my boss, Brian. But I got the sense that most of them were more interested in the sights of London than getting their hands dirty digging into our business. Brian stayed at The Intercontinental Hotel on Piccadilly when he visited and suggested I should rent a fully serviced apartment nearby the office so that other visitors from San Francisco could use that instead of expensive hotel accommodation. I did a quick search and showed him what was available and he selected a plush two-bed apartment at the top of Whitehall, just off Trafalgar Square. It cost us £12,000 a month and I don't recall any visitors from across the pond ever staying there! That's not to say I didn't, as it saved me the boring commute. Often others in the office would stay, too, as we did work some quite unbelievable hours.

Everything was going really well and we were very much on schedule with our launch. Nathan and his team had designed (within corporate guidelines) and developed a quite brilliant front end interface (what a customer would use) that even today, over 20 years later, wouldn't look out of place. The office was a mine of activity - all very informal but a tremendous collective effort. I was immensely proud of what we accomplished and, by December 2000, we were issuing test cards to staff and putting the finishing touches to everything prior to launching the following Spring.

Before Christmas I attended a big 'Cards International' awards event at The Grosvenor in Park Lane and was delighted to walk away with the award for best new Credit Card of the year. From that point the company was now firmly in the spotlight for sure and my job was increasingly becoming that of an ambassador to the media, other financial institutions, IT businesses and vast numbers of companies who wanted to get in on the dot-com boom. The other major development around this time was my boss changed. Brian was more an investor than an out and out banker and the new guy, Jim Harris, was a hands on business leader.

In early 2001, I was caught completely by surprise when one night Jim called me and asked if I could meet him at the Intercontinental for breakfast the next morning at 07.30. I didn't even know he was in the country, but obviously something was wrong and I was damned if I could think what. The next morning I walked into the Intercontinental restaurant, saw Jim, but also the VP of HR. Now, this was serious. I racked my brains as I walked gingerly towards them; I knew I had done nothing wrong, nothing that warranted this. Jim was very cordial and engaged in small talk but I cut across him and said I thought it would be sensible if he got to the point, so he did. The US business had come under scrutiny from the FDIC (not dissimilar to the UK Financial Conduct Authority), which had exposed a risk insofar as the business wasn't making sufficient provisions for bad debt – they had identified a hole of tens of millions of dollars. Although the company was awash with cash, it didn't have that much to call on and so they were frantically running around trying to raise more capital. They couldn't go to the shareholders again as they had recently completed a major round of funding so options were limited. One thing was for sure, they most certainly couldn't afford to be launching a card in a new country as the more successful it was, the more initial cost would need to be covered.

Harris told me the business was going to be 'put on ice'

for 12-15 months and I would have to let most of the staff go. There was a list of about 12 of us who they wanted to relocate to the US and work there until it could return and launch in the UK. Jim asked me if I thought those identified would be willing to temporarily relocate and I replied that I had no idea but I suspected not - and I told him that I would not do so. He suggested he might consider keeping me employed in the UK as their 'spokesman' but, to be frank, I wasn't entertaining such thoughts at that particular moment. All the time the thought of my share options were front of mind but my instincts told me there was much more to this than met the eye and my instincts rarely, if ever, let me down.

The calculation of provision for bad debt was another Haufin responsibility. It's actually not rocket science - at its simplest you just take the money in arrears at each checkpoint (typically every 30 days up to the point of write off which in in our case was nine months) and what proportion of that ends up getting written off at that time. For example, if 1% of the money that becomes 30 days overdue is written off, then every month a business will take the aggregate balances of its accounts at 30 days and allocate 1% of that to its loss provision (a giant pot of money to pay for future losses). It's dynamic and moves up and down as the performance of the portfolio changes. Anyway Haufin, who was a bit of a darling among senior management, had royally cocked up by introducing a quite different way of calculating how much was needed but, worse than that, it became apparent that she and Harris as well as others had knowingly made accounting adjustments to hide the delinquencies (overdue accounts) and bad debt. They were later accused of insider trading, essentially selling off their shares in the business, knowing that the financial health wasn't as reported. While I'm sure it didn't start out that way, it ended as a massive shitshow where a small number of people screwed up a brilliant business and then sought to profit (and presumably make their escape) before it all came crashing down.

The breakfast meeting lasted about an hour and not a lot more detail was given. I grilled him on how on earth they could have allowed such a thing to happen but his response was far from convincing and he was most certainly very uncomfortable. He wrapped up by about 09.00, asking me to assemble all the staff at the Cafe Royal in Piccadilly at 10.00, when he would make the announcement. I walked slowly back to the offices in a state of confusion. There was no indication whatsoever of any difficulties at corporate level and I assume the FDIC resolution was both unexpected and swift.

I deliberately didn't return to the office until about five minutes before everyone would need to leave to be ready for 10.00. I quickly walked through the offices telling everyone to log off, put their phones on busy and make their way up to the Cafe Royal for an announcement by Harris. I didn't let on at all and I was really quite distressed to hear as we walked up that the speculation was that Harris was here to congratulate us on our brilliant work and quite likely to be awarding big bonuses for our collective achievement. I walked with Eileen and I didn't even tell her, only that it wasn't good news.

As soon as we got to The Cafe Royal it was probably clear to everyone that the news wasn't going to be good. There were two security people on the door, Harris and the HR fella were on the stage, and another five security people were placed around the room, all looking very mean! Harris asked me to sit on the stage with him but I was having none of it, I politely declined and sat with everyone else. He dithered around a bit telling everyone what a wonderful job they had done and then got to the point, he continued to try and sugarcoat it, but there's no nice way to tell people they had lost their job.

Then came the unexpected bit: nobody was able to return to the office immediately and there was a list posted by the door with everyone's names on. Essentially, they were going to let people in five at a time and they then had 10 minutes to collect their personal belongings and a letter telling them what their severance would be. The business was clearly paranoid about having its IP (intellectual property) taken, so everyone was under great scrutiny. Harris and Co then made a speedy escape and I was left to try and handle all the questions and to console those who needed it. The first five had to go to the office and so I told everyone else to go to the pub we often used just off Lower Regent Street and that's where we could do our talking. We made our way there very quietly and solemnly - it reminded me of a funeral procession.

The pub was quite an experience. Lots of obvious bad feeling and quite a few tears too. I put my business credit card behind the bar and told everyone to order whatever the hell they wanted, which they did. Shortly after we arrived the first five who went to the office came in and gave us their account. It wasn't pleasant and they were watched like hawks. All the laptops had been taken out while we were in Cafe Royal and all they could do was pick up their personal possessions. Their severance letters didn't say much other than they were to be paid three months' notice and that was it. This went on all day. I think we arrived in the pub about 11.00 and the last group didn't go down to the offices until about 16.00. I actually took great delight in the fact that none of the 12 that were offered jobs back in San Francisco accepted them - it made me feel proud in a bizarre way. I didn't go into the office as I had already arranged to meet Harris the following day.

By mid afternoon, not only was the pub full of us from EnCard, there were at least half a dozen recruiters doing the rounds of everyone. We had built a solid reputation and the vultures were circling. Most wouldn't have any difficulty at all getting work and would be in jobs within a week but I felt sad for the 'generalists' among the group who would have to work a bit harder. But the employment market was strong and I doubted any would be unemployed for long.

As the day went on and the alcohol flowed the atmosphere lightened and, by about 18.00, it was like a scene from a very boisterous wedding! People started to drift off amid all sorts of promises about reunions and staying in touch. By 19.30 there were only about half a dozen of us left and I needed to call it a day and went to pay the tab. I was actually surprised that it was only about £2,000! There was an Aberdeen Steak House on Lower Regent Street and I desperately needed to eat, so a few of us went there. We had dinner and I pulled out the business card to pay. It was declined as 'Account Blocked'!

The next day I went in to see Harris, reiterated that I wouldn't be going to San Francisco and he gave me my severance letter, which was basically six months' pay. I made a play to have all or even some of my share options either immediately vest or retained until vesting date, but was unsuccessful. It was all done in 30 minutes and I was on my way back home.

You'd think that was it, but not quite. About two weeks later I got a call from a company called iformation, it was a joint venture established between two massive blue chip businesses, Boston Consulting Group and Goldman Sachs. They asked to see me in London as soon as possible and I was there without hesitation. The business was investing heavily in dot-com start-ups, knew what we had done at EnCard and wanted to know if I would do it again. Its thinking was that it could white label it and sell (licence) it to banks across Europe, indeed it already had five banks who had registered a serious interest. I took away all the information and arranged to meet with Eileen, Brendan and Nathan and take them through it. I was concerned by the very aggressive timelines that iformation had given me and so I asked Nathan if he could get us up and running and what it would take. I should have been angry, but wasn't, when he replied that he had copied all the software we had ever developed and all he really needed to do was replace all the branding and company terminology and we'd be ready to go. So, the major time challenge was hardware and infrastructure, which Brendan would have no difficulty with. We put together a comprehensive proposal for iformation, which I took back about two weeks later and presented to them. It included our equity participation requirements, which were fairly aggressive, but we would be paid fairly modest salaries in the early days. The company didn't baulk at all, agreed and said it would need 4-6 weeks to get all the legals and structural stuff organised.

And, sadly, that's where the chapter ends. When the dot-com bubble burst, it did so in a gigantic way. Almost overnight businesses shut down and there was carnage throughout the on-line world. The markets went into freefall as investors and fund mangers literally panicked and, for no good reason whatsoever, sold off their investments – in most cases at a loss. It was all triggered by one or a few major investment business cashing in their holdings and which started a domino effect. True, over the previous 3-4 years, money had been pouring in with little emphasis on short-term returns, but history now shows that the panic was misplaced. Since then, the few that survived and those that followed, equally heavily invested in, have flourished. If you were anywhere near an internet business in 2000-2001 you'll know exactly what I am referring to – nobody was spared.

iformation called me to tell me that it was suspending all new investments and would be in touch later. They never were.

13 - POSITIVES AND NEGATIVES

Away from the highs and lows of EnCard, life was good and I was settled. I'd joined the golf club and loved seeing the girls every other weekend and many other times. In the summer of 2000, when Fran was seven and Steph five, I took them to Menorca for a week. On the flight, I noticed a lady with two young girls about the same ages as mine. She was attractive, but she stood out because she was tall. When we got to the hotel, the girls wanted to do what all children of their ages would want to - go straight to the pool. They were soon splashing around and before long, I spotted the lady from the flight sat by the pool with an elderly lady. Within minutes, Fran and Steph were playing with the two girls from the flight. It wasn't long before I introduced myself to Dawn and her mother.

The following two weeks followed a similar pattern: all four girls played in the pool together, while I chatted to Dawn and her mum. Dawn was a single parent and lived in Sanderstead and, coincidently, was MD of Woolwich Financial Advisers, a business unit of Woolwich Bank. So, although we had never met, we both knew of each other from my short time working there. I thought about asking her out when we got home but wasn't at all sure I wanted or needed another relationship. It was at Gatwick when we returned and were waiting for our bags at the carousel that I asked for her phone number and suggested we might get together for dinner. She agreed and we met up near to where she lived, then met up a few more times.

I had lost my job at EnCard in February 2001 and wasn't in any particular hurry to get another one. I traded my NSX for a virtually new model in silver and things with Dawn moved forward. We were getting more serious, but the journey between Sanderstead and Camberley was a bore, particularly when her job was another 30 miles beyond where she lived. We had a bit of a long distance, every other weekend, type of relationship for several months.

I had a steady flow of calls from headhunters after EnCard and one in particular took my fancy. I will call it "Prism", a business unit of a large and very well known conglomerate, with many established travel and hospitality brands. They were looking for a Senior VP and COO to run its financial services arm across Europe, based not far from Slough in Buckinghamshire. After a multi-stage interview process, I was offered and accepted the role and started immediately. The office was commutable for me, but it was 25 miles to the north west and so any remote thoughts I might have had of moving over towards Dawn simply evaporated. That decision caused something of a headache as there was no way she could commute to her work from a Camberley base. So we continued with our weekend and occasional midweek relationship, which was further complicated by our mutual responsibilities towards children.

The job was perfect. I had about 1,000 people working for me in operations, servicing, IT and marketing – of which about 600 were based in UK (split between a service centre on the south coast and Head Office) and the remainder spread fairly evenly in Paris, Hamburg, Milan and Oslo. The role was demanding from the point of view of visiting each office once a month (more, if there were issues) and so once a week I would find myself on a plane going somewhere. Very quickly – and not unsurprisingly – I realised that only two or three of my seven or eight direct reports were worth keeping, so I called Harty and after our usual 'cat and mouse' discussions I was able to bring him on board as head of product management.

Surprisingly – and what turned out to be fatally – my boss quit after I had been there about 10 weeks and so FD Simon Walters and I ran the business for three months. The head of international (Steve Franks), who was leading the recruitment for a replacement CEO, narrowed down his candidates to two and asked me and Simon to meet them and give him our feedback.It wasn't an easy task. One of them we found to be 'wishy-washy' - a lifelong banker with very little charisma and no obvious skills to run a complex and challenging business. The other (Mike Marsden) was more qualified, had recently left a senior role at Goldman Sachs but was thoroughly unlikeable. He was really quite arrogant and, when we interviewed him, he was so sure the job was already his that he talked in an almost threatening way. I thought I might need to endorse him for my own good. Knowing Steve I suspect he had already given Mike more than a few hints that he was the preferred candidate. Simon and I were as diplomatic as possible with Steve, suggesting that Mike Marsden was the better of the two but perhaps a wider search might throw up someone even more suitable. Steve didn't want to delay longer because there was too much to be done, so Marsden showed up two weeks later - and took his seat in the top floor corner office.

I've never worked for such a thoroughly unpleasant person. Marsden took great delight in bullying people (not me) and I witnessed, on several occasions, his public castigation of what were often fairly junior employees. I made a point that if he ever did it to any of my people then I would intervene and give him what for, he never did. I vividly recall him having a junior finance lady in tears when she couldn't explain why the sales revenues were under budget. And even though the sales leader, David Scott (a very decent bloke) did his best to protect her (it wasn't her responsibility after all) Marsden took great delight in publicly grinding her into the ground.

On another occasion he told me to fire one of my marketing managers for no good reason, other than I guess he didn't like her. That led to a very unpleasant conflict with him but I prevailed and, although she did eventually leave (he made life unpleasant for her), I did manage to get her a generous severance.

Here's one story that sums up Mike Marsden. He once told the sales team to go into his former employer, Goldman Sachs, as it had recently launched a credit card and would be good candidates for partnering with us (we supplied a range of premium benefits and services to banks that they passed or sold on to their bank and credit card customers). When the sales guys went up to Canary Wharf to make their pitch, they were shown to the conference room and, on the way there, they passed an office door with a plaque saying 'This used to be Mike Marsden's office'. He only worked there for about 18 months, so to gain that sort of notoriety must have taken some going!

Very early on in my tenure I discovered a major efficiency bottleneck because all five operating centres were working on a standalone basis. I could see that there would be major financial and service delivery benefits by linking them all together and allowing workflow and call management to seamlessly transfer between centres. By making changes, we could even out the peaks and troughs of activity and allow for more accurate and efficient resourcing. I also saw the potential of opening a multilingual service centre in southern Ireland with the Irish offering enormous financial incentives to attract new businesses to their country. I put a business case together for about $20m of investment, which was approved. A fair slice of that (around $4m) would be used to purchase new telephony and one of the companies that I invited to tender was AT&T, the US equivalent of BT and, therefore, a giant in the industry.

Shortly after it had submitted its proposal, I got a call from someone at AT&T, asking if I would be interested in joining them for the 2001 Monaco Grand Prix. They were one of the sponsors of the Jaguar F1 team and were taking a few guests down. It sounded like a plush affair and I accepted, but I stressed to them that I was still going through the tender process and that I wouldn't let it influence my final decision. I let Marsden and Steve know I was going, just to be sure I was covered.

I had experienced hospitality in many forms over the years, but this trip was insanely over the top. I was flown to Nice in Club on the Friday before the race on Sunday. On arrival, I was taken by private car to the Hotel Negresco (a ridiculously opulent hotel on the Promenade des Anglais) and, later that evening, met up with the other guests and taken to dinner in a wonderful nearby restaurant by AT&T's head of Europe. The next morning we were met after breakfast, taken to the marina and transported around to Monaco in a wonderful crewed power cruiser. We moored in the harbour and went ashore to our private area, which was a huge apartment with terrace about three floors up, directly over the start/finish line. It was so close that I felt I could almost touch the cars below.

We watched the various build-up races and F1 qualifying, all the time being offered the most delightful food and wines. Once the day was over we were taken up to The Hotel du Paris where we had a private dinner in one of the wine cellars. I was sat next to Nikki Lauda and on the same table as Jackie Stewart - I can't deny I was somewhat overawed but I enjoyed it immensely. After dinner we were taken down to the harbour and a tender took us out to a large motor yacht for more drinks and social indulgence. In the main lounge area, a band was playing and I remarked to the fella next to me that they sounded an awful lot like Supertramp. "They ARE Supertramp!" he replied.

On Sunday morning, we were picked up before breakfast and again taken around to Monaco in the motor cruiser. We were dropped off and taken to the Jaguar pit area, where we were able to sit in the cars and watch the mechanics going about their business. We were then taken over to one of the giant trailers with tables set up outside and had breakfast with the drivers - Pedro de la Rosa and Eddie Irvine. Once breakfast was over, it was back to the apartment on the start/finish line, ready for lunch. When it appeared, so did Prince Albert – who introduced himself and got stuck into the prawn sandwiches. By now, I'm all at sea and wasn't prepared for him saying hello to me. What do you say to a real-life Prince and ruler of a small country? I knew he was a petrolhead and so I started talking about cars and that I owned an NSX. He smiled and, thankfully, moved on.

Once the race began, us guests were stood against the balcony wall watching intently and, as it happened, Eddie Irvine finished third – the first time in their short F1 history that one of their drivers had made the podium. The place went berserk and everyone turned to the person next to them and gave them a huge hug. I was most definitely the 'huggee' as my hugger was none other than Penny Lancaster. Rod didn't have anything to worry about, my knees turned to jelly.

I don't remember much more about that weekend – I was in shock for most of it. But I do remember making my decision on the telephony provider three weeks later – and it wasn't AT&T. Thank goodness I had properly briefed Marsden and Steve because there were several calls made by senior AT&T people in the ensuing period and life could have been tricky had I not properly laid out my stall.

Within my first year, I had replaced all of the dead wood on my team and we had successfully deployed our big technology upgrade. My first bonus was exceptionally good and I was loving life.

For Easter 2002, Dawn and I and all four girls went on

holiday to Antigua and stayed at The St James' Club. It all went pretty well, although the highlight of the 10 days was me turning a Hoby Cat completely over and sending all four girls overboard. The boat master said it was the first time he had seen one of the boats do it; the girls loved it and wanted me to do it again, but thankfully I couldn't!

By late 2002 the back and forth with Dawn was getting really tiresome – and we eventually agreed that she should move over to Camberley. The idea was she would work from home a couple of days a week, go into central London a couple of days and travel to her office in Kent for the remaining day. We both put our houses on the market and started looking. The market was fairly slow and it took some months but we got there and both had sales in the pipeline. Buying was a bit more tricky, but we came across (goodness knows how) a tiny two-bed cottage, five minutes' walk from the town centre on possibly the best road in town, private, no through and with about 10 houses. The cottage was old and in need of attention, but it was sitting on nearly an acre of completely flat land, most of which was obscured by overgrown rhododendrons. It was going to be a huge project, but we saw the potential to demolish the house and put up a large new house that we could design ourselves. We finally bought 'Pucks Cottage' in early 2003 and set about designing our new home. The cottage, later to be renamed Culzean House, was the ninth house I had owned.

Meanwhile, Marsden was becoming even more of an

ogre. For some reason, he kept dragging me, Simon and Doug Collins (HR director), to Paris for irrelevant and meaningless meetings. We were far too busy to be doing them so regularly and none of us were happy about it. It was during this period that my marketing director in Paris quit and there wasn't a natural successor, so I instructed a search to be undertaken. I was surprised when Marsden came to my office and, out of the blue, told me I should give the job to one of the marketing managers there - a lady by the name of Claudine. Now, Claudine was very nice, but was in no way whatsoever a marketing director and I told him so. But he was insistent to the point of trying to instruct me to give her the job. I refused point blank and he was not happy. It was all very odd, given that marketing was my responsibility and I was more than familiar with her skills and capabilities.

A week later he dragged us all to Paris (yet) again. We congregated in the boardroom for our all-day meeting about nothing in particular but, after about 45 minutes, Marsden's phone rang and he stepped out of the room to take the call. He returned saying he had to leave for a few hours but we should carry on. We were all pretty underwhelmed, to say the least. Immediately after he left, a break was suggested and we went to get coffees. As we passed through the building we walked past a window overlooking the back of the car park and one of us happened to look out and pointed at Marsden getting into a car with Claudine the marketing manager. We had our suspicions, but now they were confirmed. I went into the marketing area and asked if

Claudine was available, but was told that she had gone home feeling ill and wouldn't be returning that day. Marsden returned later in the afternoon, just as we were preparing to leave for the airport. He made some weak excuse about a crisis call with the US leadership team or such like – we all stayed quiet.

I had decided enough was enough and Simon, Doug and I agreed that we would take our concerns to Steve. We were due at an executive meeting in Nice a week or two later and planned on telling him then. But, a few days before Nice Steve called me and asked to meet with me in his office in London to talk through a report he was preparing on validating the business case for our recent investments. I got on well with Steve and after we had gone through what he needed and were just chatting I let rip about Marsden, his appalling management style, his (at least one) affair and the fact that he was dragging his management team around Europe to disguise his activities. Steve was pretty opaque and simply told me to leave it with him. A day or two later, Marsden called me up to his office and he was just chatting away about random stuff then opened an Autocar magazine, slid it across his desk to me with the page opened at adverts from Maranello, the Ferrari dealership in Egham. He had circled one – a Ferrari 360 for sale for £100,000 – and asked me if I would like it. "Of course," I replied and he said he'd see that I got that as my upcoming year bonus if I "kept my nose clean". I was appalled and asked him if he was serious to which he replied that he most certainly was. I tossed the magazine back to him, got up and walked out. I can't recall exactly what I said, but it certainly wasn't "Let me think about it."

Our Nice meeting went ahead and at the end of the first day Steve said he wanted all of us to meet on the terrace of his (giant) room at 07.30 for a breakfast meeting before the events of the day started. Simon, Doug and I got together later that evening and made sure we were all on the same page and that our arguments were consistent. The next morning we all met up and Seb Youlden, head of international HR was also there. Steve opened by saying that there were concerns about Mike and then asked the three of us to individually tell them what the complaint was. I went first and didn't hold back one bit. I was well prepared and well rehearsed and I told it exactly how it was. Doug was more diplomatic and circumspect, but was similarly critical and raised several different examples of his inappropriate behaviour. Next up was Simon, who was by far the longest-serving of us all and very much Steve's poster boy. I couldn't believe it – If ever I had witnessed anyone 'sitting on the fence' there here it was. He was saying things like "Mike can be a hothead at times", which was dramatically different to what we'd discussed. When asked about Mike's affair(s) (there was lots of speculation about another woman in Milan, too) Simon simply said that he was not aware of them. Marsden gave his response – total denial and that the business needed strong leadership and he was doing his job and we were trending to record profits (despite

Mike, not because of him!). Steve wrapped it up by telling us that he would consider everything he had heard and get back to us.

About two weeks later, Steve visited our offices, took over the boardroom and called all three of us in, one by one. He asked me if I was still of the same view and I told him I was. He went into a reasonable speech about how a management team needed to be a single cohesive unit, which I agreed with. He did the same with Doug and Simon, but obviously I don't know what they said. Two days later Steve asked for me and Doug to meet with him and Seb in London. We were both (very reluctantly, seemingly) fired and given a generous pay-off to soften the blow. I was very upset but I knew it was too late to appeal or protest – it simply doesn't work like that. Unsurprisingly, Simon stayed on and I'm fairly sure why, but I was at an age – and with enough experience – to know that nothing in corporate life should surprise. What was surprising, but ultimately very satisfying, was that Marsden was also fired a few days later. I never really figured out why Steve fired Doug and I. We were successful, had high-performing teams and were popular. It was an odd and very unsatisfying conclusion to 2003 and a somewhat unsatisfying period for me.

I remained pissed off about the whole thing for a while, but grateful for the money because events with the house that I had recently started building had taken an unexpected turn – so if ever the timing was right, then that was it.

14 - DEMOLISHING AND REBUILDING

In terms of rebuilding 'Pucks Cottage', we had seen a picture of a house in a magazine and it looked wonderful. Admittedly, it was just a shot of the exterior, but we decided it was what we wanted our house to look like. A friend who could put together pretty good drawings worked with me and we simply sketched out what a house might look like on the inside – it was great fun and turned out to be a relatively easy exercise. There were four girls to be considered and, knowing what children could be like, my first requirement was that all four girls' bedrooms would be exactly the same size with the same window area, so that there would be no arguments. I also wanted 'Jack and Jill' bathrooms between each of their two bedrooms. The main bedroom was to be at the back, with patio doors out to a balcony and a large walk-in wardrobe and en suite.

Downstairs, we wanted a large kitchen-diner with a play/TV room off to the side. There were to be patio doors to the garden and more doors from a large lounge at the rear. The front of house would have a big central reception area, with a study to one side and dining room to the other. The remaining space was enough for a downstairs toilet, utility room and door to the side and/ or garage. The big wow factor for me was a central solid oak staircase, which turned both ways at the top. By the time we had finished and got everything we wanted, the house ended up at a whisker under 6000 square feet.

Planning permission wasn't too difficult to obtain, taking four months and which was given in May 2003. I had been introduced to an architect who worked for a council and he drew up the plans with me and put all the detail in. Surprisingly, our sketches all worked out well and the symmetry of the house was spot on. We went for top-of-the-range materials (roof, rendering, windows, etc) and, having had a few suggestions from my Norwegian colleagues at work, went for full concrete floors up and down, which allowed us to install underfloor heating throughout the entire house. That was such a good decision, it provided a wonderful even heat and was very efficient too.

We had already identified about five potential builders, and a friend of a friend was a quantity surveyor and he put together the most comprehensive tender document, which we distributed. It took a while but eventually all five quotes were returned and I was surprised by two things. Firstly the large variation in price and secondly the absolute price – the cheapest of which was £375,000 to build a 6,000 square foot house! We examined all the quotes and found nothing untoward, so I called the one with the lowest quote and asked for a potential start date. They gave me a date in August/September 2003, three months ahead. That was OK so I then called all of the references they had provided. All were substantial property businesses and all gave a glowing reference. The business had been trading for over 30 years and, after all the due diligence I had done, I was happy to sign the contract. Dawn and I had both sold our houses and they completed within weeks of each other. We found a small three-bedroom terraced house to rent, about half a mile away from the site of the new house, ideal for keeping an eye on the building work.

Around this time, Karen met a new boyfriend (Steve) and, after a short period renting a house together nearby to where she lived, they decided to sell their respective properties and buy a house in Cranleigh. That made my life (and that of the girls in the context of their time with me) a whole lot easier as it was only about 40 minutes away. I had met Steve a couple of times, he seemed decent enough and I thought it would be a good move for the girls. I think the move coincided with Fran moving up to senior school and both the primary and secondary schools were nearby to where they were moving to, so everything worked out well for them all.

I lost my job around the time that building work on the new house started, which I suppose was good timing. I was in no hurry to get another job and thought it would be beneficial to be available while the house was being built, so that everything went to plan and I was on the spot to answer the inevitable questions. I treated myself to a new car, a three-year-old Ferrari 355 in 'Monte Carlo Blue'. I thought it would occupy me when the house didn't.

In October 2003, the house was demolished and the site was cleared in days. I then got in landscapers who completely cleared the plot, all bar about the last 30 yards of garden. Down there were magnificent Scots pines and we planned to create a border of acers and leave the bottom end wild, while turfing the rest.

I visited the site a couple of times a week and got to know the foreman well. By the end of November, the foundations were in and the first courses of blockwork were appearing. Everything was looking good and the plan to be moving in around April/May 2004 was well on track. I found watching the progress of work really interesting and I was soon visiting the site every day – looking around and imagining how it would end up.

One particular Monday, I got down to the site around mid-morning and was surprised to see no activity and only one vehicle in the driveway. The foreman was stood by his car and on the phone. When he saw me, he hung up. He looked unhappy and I quickly realised why. His firm had gone bust overnight. Well, not 'bust' but the owner had simply disappeared and emptied the business bank account of every penny. On top of that, the owner had been using the good name of the business to run up huge accounts with building suppliers and seemingly owed a vast amount of money. He speculated that the owner had disappeared with – and owing – several millions of pounds. I was in a state of absolute shock and asked the foreman how it could happen to such a reputable business with over 30 years of history. It was only then that I learned that the business had been sold the previous year by the original owner and the new guy was someone who had something of an unknown past. It quickly became clear to me that this new owner had purchased the business with the express intent of doing what he did. I suppose it was a pretty clever thing to do, but he left individuals and businesses in a highly distressed position. I desperately hoped that he would be tracked down and dealt with. For my part, I was now in huge difficulty.

I told the foreman to go home and I would be in touch. The first thing I did was call a couple of the other builders who had quoted and asked them if they could take over the job. Both were willing but said that they couldn't start for several months, which didn't work for me at all.

Then I came up with an idea. I called the foreman and suggested that I employ him and his team through my consulting company that I had set up for whenever I might take on short-term consulting projects. His job would be to manage the tradesmen and also order all the materials and supplies that we needed to complete the house. He agreed and I was able to open trade accounts at the big suppliers I needed. Two weeks later we started work again – this time with me being very hands-on, in fact, it became my full-time job for the next six months.

One of the first problems I ran into were with costs. It became quickly apparent that, in order to win the contract, the owner of the building company had submitted prices for materials that weren't achievable. For example, he quoted around £14,000 for plasterboard and fixings but when I met with the plasterboard company it showed me they had quoted him around £23,000. The same was true for many other elements of work such as roof tiling, rendering and much of the plumbing and fixtures and fittings. When I went through the whole thing, it looked like the actual cost to complete would be about £70,000 more than I had budgeted. Naturally, I wasn't happy and spent a considerable amount of time renegotiating costs and had to be really hard nosed in most cases. I gave the suppliers the option of either reducing their prices or not doing any business with me. I also offered to make cash payments, which worked better than I expected. On top of that I used 'my' tradespeople for more work than originally planned, partly because it was important to keep them occupied full-time.

To cut a long story short, I somehow managed to

complete the house on budget and, quite apart from finishing the build, I was immensely proud of keeping the finances in check. The house and all the landscaping was completed in May 2004 and it was beautiful – to me, anyway! It drew lots of attention and we had more than one estate agent wanting to look around simply out of curiosity. We even had the local paper call me up and ask to look around and get my story; I declined.

For someone that has difficulty with even the simplest maintenance, I really felt we had achieved something. It was hard and although we didn't actually lay bricks or cut pipes – or do any of the labour – simply managing and coordinating a variety of trades and suppliers to make sure the job was done to the highest standard took a huge amount of effort. It certainly paid dividends. When the house was sold a few years later, the agent handling it told us that it was the most expensive house ever sold in Camberley – something else that I took some delight in knowing.

In my downtime from house building I discovered online poker, which was in its infancy, but growing very quickly. I've tried to explain to some people that tournament poker is not gambling in the same way as roulette, slot machines or blackjack – it is more a game of high skill. While there is, of course, an element of luck (the cards that one is dealt) the cards that are dealt are only one of several elements of the game. As a very good poker pro once said: "It's not what you get dealt, it's what you can have others think you have been dealt".

Some people, though, are simply prejudiced and would not open their minds to my argument. Anyway, I studied the game of 'No Limit Hold 'Em' and signed up with Ladbrokes and played in several on-line tournaments. I found myself doing exceptionally well and winning some very decent prize money. I enjoyed the game immensely and got to make some really good friends in the virtual world (such names as Crippin, BigAdzC, Skalie, Sudsy, Banksoir7, Richlizard, Strummer7, Action Jack and many many more), many who became friends in the real world. I would play in tournaments and get to know the style of many of the regular players, and developed strategies to try and keep one step ahead of them. The players came from across Europe and beyond and in those early days the Swedish were there in big numbers. They were pretty fearless in the way they played, but I found I was able to hold my own and beat many of their big name players. It was a good way of relaxing between the many difficulties and stresses of building the house.

My first win of note was actually a satellite into a bigger live tournament. A satellite is a game where an entry fee is paid and one in 10 will progress to the next event stage. I paid a $100 entry and there were about 30 players. I ended in the top three, so went through to the next stage, which was a $1,000 entry. In that tournament, there were about 20 players and the top two won a $10,000 entry to a poker cruise, which was in the Caribbean in January 2005 – I got through. The prize was broken down into a $5,500 entry to the tournament on the ship and the other $4,500 was for the cost of the seven-day cruise for two (Dawn would come) plus travel expenses.

I also encouraged a couple of good friends Tony Burchett, who I had become good friends with whilst at Amex, and Paul Soper to try and qualify too and I was delighted that over the next month they were both successful. By the time the entries closed in late December, Ladbrokes had nearly 400 players qualified leading to a tournament with a prize pool of nearly $2m. As I recall the prize money was paid the first 100 players, with $350,000 for the winner down to about $8,000 for 100th place. It was highly memorable and very enjoyable. There was a great atmosphere on the ship and everyone was very friendly but, it was the first time I had ever played live poker and I was really nervous too.

The tournament ended up running for over four days. Each day it would start around 4.00pm and run through until about 2.00am. Seeing 400 players in a room seated at tables of nine all rattling about 50,000 chips each was quite intimidating for a newbie but, after a few hours of not getting too involved and mostly observing, I started to settle. I made it through day one, by which time about 150 had been eliminated and the next day I was still there at the end and we were down to just over 100 players who would start day three.

By day three, things were getting very tense as we were nearing the magic 100th when prize money would kick in. Play was tightening up as nobody wanted to be eliminated so near to getting into the prize money. I recall vividly when there were 101 players left (it's called the bubble, the next player out gets nothing but everyone else will get prize money). I was dealt a pair of Aces, which is the very highest hand – although still beatable – and, after a round of betting there were just two of us playing the hand. I wanted it over quickly and not take any chances, so after a bet and raise from my opponent I went 'all in' meaning I put every single chip I had into the pot as a bet. I expected him to fold instantly and we would move on to the next hand, but he didn't. He thought and thought and thought more. I was worried, I knew I had the best hand but didn't want to take any risk, even though I might be a 3/1 or 4/1 favourite. Eventually – and after the tournament director said he had no more time to make a decision – he folded his hand and showed me he had a pair of Queens. Shortly afterwards a player was eliminated, which brought a loud cheer from those remaining. We had all just won a minimum of $8,000.

Towards the end of day three we were down to about 30 players. I was sitting about eighth or ninth in the rankings and was dealt Ace, King – both hearts and in the first round of betting there was only me and one opponent betting and raising each other. I was sure my hand was good and ended up putting all of my chips in and was surprised when he called me, but delighted when he turned over his Ace King but both of different suits. I was the marginal favourite as the chances were, when the five 'community' cards were dealt, we would both have the same hand, but because I had two cards of the same suit to start with I had the possibility of making a 'flush', (five cards of the same suit). The dealer laid down the five community cards one by one and I was horrified to see the first three were all clubs and one of his cards was a club. The fourth card was a diamond but the fifth a club, so he made the most improbable flush and I was beaten.

The dealer counted our respective chips. I was broken - had I won that hand I would have been sitting in first, second or third place, but now I was probably out. After a count of our chips it turned out that I had a few more chips than my opponent so I get a few back - enough to play one hand but probably not enough to worry anyone. I actually put them all in without even looking at my cards. By some magic I managed to win the hand and the very next hand I got dealt two threes, they're not good either, but I put all my chips in again. I'm not surprised to get two callers but when the community cards are dealt another three appears and I win the pot! I have somehow got myself back in the game and slowly I manage to build my chips back up.

The day ended with just six players left in - and, miraculously, I am one of them. The draw is made for seats the next day and I am in seat six and in seat five is 'Skalie' a very well-known professional who is probably the favourite to win.

The final day's play was actually a couple of days

away so I had plenty of time to think about my tactics and unwind with Burchett and Soper at our next two stops, British Virgin Islands and Aruba. Ladbrokes tell us the final six will be introduced to the 700+ audience one by one and we will enter the stage to music of our choosing. Burchett and Soper chose mine for me: 'Is this the way to Amarillo?'. The next day on the beach we rehearse what will be my entrance, to the amusement of the onlookers. I get advice from almost everyone and the general consensus was that if everyone folded their cards round to Skalie and he put a bet in then I should raise him as he was a notoriously aggressive player when in the right seat position (relative to the dealer), meaning he would put big bets in on marginal hands.

Two days later and the remaining six were called down one by one in front of 700-800 spectators in the ship's theatre. Everything was being filmed and prominent poker tournament commentator Jesse May is doing the introductions and commentary. We sat down, the formalities behind us and I ordered a Corona to help calm the nerves. The first hand of the day was dealt. As almost expected the first four all folded their hands and Skalie put in a fairly big bet. I looked at my cards and saw I had a King and a Queen, which is a premium hand and only really behind to a pair of Aces, Kings or Queens – or Ace King or Ace Queen. I looked him over and was convinced he was bluffing. If it were anyone else I think I would have just called his bet, but as it was Skalie I announced 'All In' and put every chip I had into the pot, confident that he would fold. He didn't. Instead he called my bet and turned over Ace King. I'm pretty well doomed and need to hit a Queen in the five community cards, but I fail to do so and I am knocked out in sixth place. I feel a bit daft having gone through all the pre-game build up and announcements, just to play one hand, but that's poker. My prize money was $75,000, which I thought was pretty good for my very first live poker tournament. I never did get my Corona though!

When I got home I used the prize money to upgrade the Ferrari. Trading in the 355 for a six-month-old 360 Spyder. I was clearly now enjoying the childhood I had missed out on.

My poker went from strength to strength and, later that year, I played in my first World Championships (World Series of Poker) in Las Vegas. It's an incredible festival with about 80 or so tournaments held over six weeks and culminating in the main event, which is a $10,000 buy in. Like the cruise I got in via a satellite (a qualifying tournament) and had all expenses paid, entry fee, flights, seven nights at The Wynn, a dedicated Ladbrokes players lounge and a lot of partying. The main event was the most awesome sight and no amount of description could do it justice if you hadn't witnessed it. The 'room' where we played in The Rio hotel holds about 3,500 people at around 400 tables. There are nearly 9,000 entrants so the first day is split over three days, so that everyone can start. Even then day two still has nearly 5,000 remaining and so an overspill hall was used. It was - and may well still be – the richest prize for the winner of any event in the world. First prize that year was a little over $12m and a total prize pool of over $90m. The first 2,300 got into the prize money but, alas, I didn't make it. I actually went to the world championships for the next four years but didn't do too well. I put that down to the draw of all the other attractions on offer and my inability to concentrate with all that was going on including the outstanding partying that Ladbrokes laid on. Those people really knew how to do it in style.

I was enjoying life – not working, or needing to work, doing well at poker and playing with my car, everything was going well. One day a good friend called me saying his brother Jason had set up a business to import electric golf trolleys from China. He had got the product developed (essentially taking a trolley to China which they used as a 'template' to build their own), developed some branding and images, and figured out how the how the supply chain (ordering, shipping, delivery) would work. But Jason didn't have the money to fulfil an initial order or undertake any sales or marketing and needed £20,000 and he asked if I would lend it to him. I knew Jason well, he was a bit of a 'scally' and I was dubious but I said I would go over to his office/warehouse (little more than a shack on a run down trading estate near Horsham), take a look and think it through.

Jason had little commercial experience, indeed his one previous business venture was a total disaster, not because it wasn't a good business but because of ill discipline. But I went over and met him and realised immediately there was great potential. He would be able to 'land' the trolleys into the UK for an all up cost of about £120, that included the cost to buy, shipping, duties and delivery from port to warehouse, everything. The only competitor at that time sold their product for around £300 so there was a great opportunity to undercut them. The trolleys would arrive in a container all nicely boxed with extensive branding and all that was really needed was for a courier label to be attached. I told Bob that I would invest £20,000 and more to get the stock that I believed was needed, but on the understanding that I would also work in the business and take on all responsibility for Sales, Marketing and Finance. His job would be to deal with the manufacturer, evolve the product and most importantly ensure what we would be getting was of the highest quality. I knew that the quality of much that was coming from China at that time was questionable to say the least.

We got up and running with an initial order of 200 trolleys and I first put them on ebay to test pricing and interest. I put our first 5 on for auction, as well as applying a £199 'Buy it Now' price. They sold immediately and all for within a few £'s of £199. The same happened the next day, and the next. I quickly realised we were on to a winner, indeed I removed the 'Buy it Now' price after a few days and the selling price settled around the £230-240 mark, clearing us a good £100 profit per trolley. I then bought space in the popular golf magazines, designed a few ad's and before we knew it our stock was all but gone. I quickly ordered up another 200 and they were selling like hot cakes too. I estimated we could easily sell 300-400 a month and there were great opportunities to develop the trolley (accessories, remote control etc) which would give us longevity. I told Jason he needed to get out to China and get into bed (not literally) with their owners, secure our relationship and put some quality mechanisms and process in place. He wasn't thrilled and despite the opportunity that was clearly presenting itself I had to pretty well kick him over there. We had sold out our 2nd batch of 200 and so I ordered up another 500. Such was the popularity of the trolley that we had pre-sold pretty well every one by the time they arrived at the warehouse and I recall a frantic 2-3 days of labelling everything up, producing paperwork and processing card payments. Jason had returned from China and it was quite clear he had done a hopeless job, he seemed to have spent most of the 3-4 days there either drunk (he said that's what the Chinese did) or on the phone to his girlfriend back home (as evidenced by the £600 expense claim he expected me to pay). I was quickly coming to the conclusion that our partnership was going to be temporary but I didn't appreciate just how right I was about that.

When the batch of 500 arrived we got all the pre-sold ones shipped out in about 3 days. We were left with about 60 and so I put in another order for 500 (there was a 6-7 week lead time on orders). I was taking a well earned rest a day or two later when the phone rang, it was a customer who had just used their trolley for the first time and the wheel bearings were really noisy and then seized up completely half way round the course. I apologised, told him how to get it back to us free of charge and a replacement would be sent. I didn't think much of it, we got the odd rogue one but I had another call with the same problem an hour or so later ….. then another, then another.

The next morning I came in and the phone was ringing off the hook. It didn't need Einstein to figure out the entire batch we had sold were not fit for purpose. The initial ones came back and I got an engineer to inspect them and his appraisal was devastating. They possibly could be made good, but the cost to do so (Including couriers and parts) would be far greater than our profit. He said that the quality of much of the materials was shocking and the assembly equally bad. Interestingly he compared it to one we had from an earlier shipment and he said there was little comparison, it appeared the factory had simply 'had us over', a classic bait and switch. I remember having the argument with Jason but what I didn't expect was for him to then disappear off the face of the earth, but that's what happened, he just upped and went. I tried to field the calls and complaints for the next few days but I was 'swimming against the tide' and fighting a losing battle. I repaid as many people as I could and when the phone eventually stopped ringing I transferred the meagre remains of what was left in the bank to my personal account, locked the door to the warehouse and walked away. Thankfully the lease for the premises was solely in Jason's name so the landlords could try and find him. I liquidated the business as best I could, tricky when one Director had disappeared, but did so properly. I lost my £20,000, and more, repaying those customers that had returned their trolleys and I suspect there were others who ran into issues down the line. That didn't sit well on my conscience. I tried to track Jason down but gave up in the knowledge that even if I did find him it would achieve nothing. It was disappointing that such a great business opportunity could be so unnecessarily screwed up.

In the scheme of things the business failure was little more than an irritation. Going into it wasn't something I needed or expected and so I 'put it down to experience' life is far too short to carry the burden of such things.

Back at home I had encouraged the girls to join Camberley Athletics Club and they used to come training every Tuesday night. I took them to competitions most weekends and enjoyed watching them, often being entered into (field) events that they had no experience of or expertise in, simply because there was nobody else to pick. I admired the way they always gave 100% even when they had no chance whatsoever.

The Tuesday training was only an hour and sometimes Karen would bring them over and either go shopping or sit in the car waiting for them. Sometimes I would meet her in a pub if there was anything to talk about in regard to the girls. One time she asked me to meet her and I thought nothing of it, but then she dropped a bombshell. She had married Steve a month or so earlier and now she told me she was moving to the USA, as he had got a job in California in precisely the place we had lived some years earlier. I was horrified and told Karen that she couldn't just up and away with my children, that I had equal rights and she couldn't simply deprive me of my right to be a father. She was not really concerned by my worries and I guess I couldn't really blame her – she had her life to lead and was hardly going to leave the girls behind. Karen suggested I could have the girls every school holiday but it simply wasn't practical and would not, in any way, make up for the loss of day-to-day and week-to-week contact. Naturally I checked my position and after a lengthy process it was determined that it was just one of those situations that couldn't be compromised on. Steve went off to his new job a few weeks later and Karen was going to follow in August (five months later) at the end of the school year.

I have struggled with the notion of God. I'm by no means an Atheist but I am agnostic. I've been trying to understand more since I was diagnosed with my disease – and have attended church and read a little. But I struggle to understand why all the evidence is from 2,000 years ago and, if there is someone watching over us, why is there so much suffering in the world today. If there were a God, could he not perform a miracle or two now and show us he is looking over us and protecting us (the human race). I have never experienced a miracle – but then maybe I have?

It might not mean much to anyone else but 'losing' my children was something that tore me apart as much as anything had ever done. If it wasn't a miracle, then the nearest I have ever got to one was when, two or three months later, Karen called me to say that Steve had lost his job in California. Therefore he would lose his resident status and would be returning home, their plans to emigrate would have to be shelved. While I most certainly felt bad for her, as I know she was excited at the prospect, I cannot describe my immense feeling of relief that my girls would be staying 'home'. Miracle or not, I had just experienced something that has been an enduring memory ever since.

15 - ALL CHANGE

Having survived the arduous ordeal of nearly losing my children, I settled back into my comfortable life with very little to complain about. I absolutely loved the house and I felt a huge sense of pride pretty well every time I went in or out of the front door. That might not make sense to anyone unless you had been responsible for – and had physically managed – every single aspect of a project such as that from day one. However, I know the love of the house and the lifestyle that I had managed to achieve masked other issues that would come home to roost.

In late 2005 I got a call from an Aussie fella that I occasionally worked with when I was in California. Geoff Cope was now CEO of GE Capital in London, they were the largest issuer of store cards in the UK. GE Capital cards were used by over 10m consumers at many of the leading high street retailers. Geoff wanted me to come in as an independent consultant and undertake a strategic review of the business, produce plans for change and then put those plans through the early stages of implementation, after which internal teams would take over. I would have a team of eight internal people and we would work alongside four McKinsey consultants. He proposed a contract term of 15 months. I wasn't sure I was ready to go back to work but he offered me a most attractive day rate and incredible bonus on completion, almost enough to allow me to retire once completed, I simply couldn't say no.

I started work shortly after, in their offices on The Strand opposite Charing Cross police station and soon figured out the cornerstones of what the strategy should look like. Most of the 10m customers were unprofitable because they either spent rarely, or didn't build up a debit balance and therefore didn't pay interest. So the solution was simple (and I'm sure Geoff already knew this): to build a range of financial products such as loans, mortgages and general insurance and cross sell those to different target audiences within the customer base.

Although I intimately understood the strategic direction GE needed to pursue, I knew it would need to be well pitched to the executive team to get agreement and, more importantly the £30m or so that I thought it needed to get it up and running. So I had my team and those from McKinsey undertake extensive research to validate and legitimise my thinking. We put together the most compelling proposal and took it to executive team, where it was unanimously approved.

The build/buy period started and was due to run for about two years. I had spent the last three or four months working between the office and home and I had the teams working very productively. I was in an area of such familiarity I could have moved much quicker, but I had a business to bring along with me and that slowed things up. My work was largely monitoring, internal PR and reporting, while steering the teams on their various courses. We got to the end of the 15 months and everything was on track and I exited the business as planned and with a very sizeable bonus that was more than generous for what I had done. It was and remained the most lucrative work I had ever done. Sadly, I watched from the outside as the program of work slowly ground to a halt. Geoff left the business and ultimately nothing was ever really accomplished. I do often wonder at the ineptitude of big corporates and how they ever managed to get where they are. It often comes down to the one individual at the helm I think.

By mid-2007 we were facing some challenges at home, specifically my relationship with Dawn's children, how things worked, our mutual roles (Dawn and I) and where the lines were to be drawn. I'll say right now that they were good children but I struggled in the role of 'stepfather' with very little experience, and certainly no 'education'. It impacted my demeanour and obviously our own relationship; things were becoming difficult. I tried to work on it but, as the children got older, things became even more difficult rather than easier as I had wrongly hoped for.

I was in a bit of a fix. I wasn't working and although I was comfortable financially, Dawn had also given up work. I had hardly been conserving monies, partly in the knowledge that once we both hit 55 we had pensions that we could access – Dawn's was a particularly generous, defined benefit pension from the Woolwich as a result of her senior position and 25+ years of service.

When Burchett's wife (Andrea) called me and asked if I would be prepared to help her with her work at British Airways (she worked with Air Miles) I knew that it would give me back full financial independence and I knew I needed that. She talked me through the challenge – basically, the teams looking after all of the global partnerships were in some disarray, revenues weren't hitting targets and the 30-strong department needed major surgery. After a couple of meetings I agreed to join, but only on a freelance basis, which she agreed to.

I started work there (Crawley, or Gatwick Airport as I preferred to think of it) in August 2007. I commuted back and forth around the M25/M23 for the next six months but, not only was the journey tough, things at home weren't improving.

I found the job fairly straightforward: I switched out some of the key people and hired replacements who weren't carrying the baggage of the past. I also restructured the teams to give better accountability and it was a fairly simple task to get things going. On top of that, a major deal was struck with Lloyds Bank to issue Air Miles on a new credit card and that boosted revenues substantially.

I recruited Anya, an external hire who had plenty of relevant Financial Services experience and assigned her to manage the Lloyds relationship, she did a superb job. I became good friends with her and still am. She has a fabulous and caring husband Andy and a lovely daughter, Lyla. Anya is a trojan who made my life so much easier at that time. I also got one of the guys who worked at Prism to take on another of the key business relationships and he did a great job too. Finally, I hired a couple of others to take over the remaining key areas of partnership management and we turned things around pretty quickly. It wasn't too difficult, it just needed some focus and determination. Within a year we were flying and smashing all of our targets.

At that time I was still playing poker and doing well. I harboured thoughts of turning professional, but the game was definitely getting harder as more, very smart, people got into it. Nevertheless, I was well ahead and, in 2007, I had a crack at The Poker Million, a big televised tournament with an entry fee of £25,000. If I could win through satellites and get to the actual competition, it was a simple winner take all game of six players in six heats. The winner of each heat was guaranteed a minimum £100,000 with the winner of the final getting £1m. But there were literally thousands of people trying to qualify, so it was going to be a challenge. I tried a couple of $100 satellites but failed and then I managed to win through to a $2,500 satellite where one in 10 would win a seat. I remember there were 17 players, so there would be a seat for the winner and they then gave second and third place people prize money of the $17,500 'leftovers'. I won and confirmed my seat in heat three, to be held at Sky's studios in Isleworth 10 weeks later.

I remember the day well! I had arranged to meet Burchett and Willsy at Waterloo for 'lunch'. We met at 11.30 and I had to be at Sky at 3.00pm, ready for the game which started at 4.00pm. Unfortunately, we were a little too excited by the occasion and wherever it was we had lunch, I drank far too much. We got the train out to Isleworth and we even stopped at a pub on the way to the studios and have another couple. By the time we got to our destination we were late and I definitely wasn't fully compos mentis. I was taken to makeup while Burchett and Willsy went to the green room. The first thing the makeup lady said to me was "Didn't anyone tell you not to wear bright colours?" I was wearing a pink shirt, which seemingly wasn't good for the cameras. As she was trying to make me look human she chatted away and told me that the final the previous year had attracted 8m viewers world wide, I think it was the first time I had felt nerves all day, thanks mostly to the effects of alcohol. I drank copious amounts of water in an effort to sober up but I also needed to be cognisant of the fact that breaks during the game were limited.

After makeup, we entered the room where the game was to be filmed, met the director and commentators and, most importantly, my competition. I already knew who they were: three known professionals (all Irish) and two other qualifiers, both of whom I had come across, one of them I had no concern about, but the other was a very good player. At this level, it wasn't going to be easy. I got off to a good start and very soon I was well focussed and composed. At the first break after about 90 minutes, I held the second highest chips and had personally knocked two of the professionals out. The commentators (as I saw when the programme was aired) were full of compliments and suggested I was possibly their favourite to win. In the next hour, the weakest of the qualifiers went out leaving me with one qualifier (the tricky one) and one professional. I ran into a bad patch, lost a decent amount of chips but still had plenty to recover and was far from out of it.

The crunch hand came when I was dealt Ace Nine of clubs, I'm 2nd to go and the first player folded his cards leaving me facing the pro. I'm fairly short stacked and so I announce 'all in' and push my chips over the line. He snap calls me and turns over a pair of 7's. This is a classic 50/50 hand, statistically it could go either way. The dealer deals out the 5 community cards and unfortunately none are an Ace or Nine and there aren't the three clubs I need to make a flush and so I am eliminated. I'm really quite miffed, in the previous 15 or so hands the pro had won two or three by getting extremely lucky and, in my view deserved to have been knocked out earlier. That's about as good an example of sour grapes as you'll find, I've gotten over it now! At the time though I was furious, not just for being eliminated but because I had played really well early on and then made a couple of mistakes which left me a little short, otherwise I'm sure I could have had him at some point. The interview immediately afterwards took about four takes as I struggled to compose myself and was repeatedly reminded that swearing was not acceptable. I struggled to get beyond the question 'Did you enjoy it' because they weren't happy with my replying 'No'. However, it was a great experience and one that I am glad I had the opportunity to participate in. As it happened the fella that knocked me out went on to win the entire thing – and a cool one million.

Back at home though, life wasn't getting better, I found it so difficult to establish a decent and productive relationship with Dawn's girls (my responsibility not theirs) and it caused conflicts between Dawn and I that I knew were of my making and made me, indeed both of us unhappy. It was late in 2007 when I told Dawn that I had to leave. I didn't feel good about it, knowing that I had failed and I was sad to give up what should have been a good relationship and also the house and life that we had established. But I knew it was for the best and for her sake as much as mine. It was sad time, we had both invested a lot into those 7 years.

Reluctantly I put the the Ferrari up for sale. My life was about to change and I knew that not only would I not have a secure place to keep it, but working full-time would give me limited opportunity to use it. I advertised it and I got a call a day later from a youngish sounding man, who came to see it on a Friday afternoon. I picked him up from the station and we went for a drive. I was really surprised how young he was and discovered he was 22. I assumed he might want to go away and think it through but he decided he wanted the car there and then, asking if we could go to the bank and he would transfer the money immediately. I was so reluctant, I had hoped for one more good weekend, but I was getting a good price so I agreed. While waiting in the bank, I asked him what he did for a living, because it was a lot of money for a youngster. The way he described it was amusing. He asked me if I knew what SAP was and I told him that I knew it was some kind of enterprise software used by many big companies. He nodded his head and said: "If you assume SAP is this big [he stretched his arms out wide], then I know this much [holding one finger up], but I know it really well". I made a few calls later and discovered that a good SAP consultant in 2007 would be making £1,500 a day. He made the transfer in the bank and I reluctantly handed over the keys. He then asked me if I had a cover for the car. I told him I didn't and asked him why he would want one? Seemingly he lived in Canary Wharf/Wapping and didn't have a garage, so it would be parked on the street. I suggested he immediately went and rented a garage!

16 - MISMATCH.COM

When I reflect on my life, I have mixed feelings. I've been very successful in many ways and a less so in others, but I always ended up with more positives than negatives. I've experienced the lows but have learnt how to pick myself up and dust myself down. The low times have been short and limited and I have had so many wonderful times that I feel very privileged to have experienced. The icing on the cake are my two wonderful girls and my equally wonderful wife who has given me such huge support. She deserved better than me but she has stuck with me and I am so truly grateful for that.

I went through one of those low points in 2008 when I was feeling pretty miserable. I had moved out of Culzean House, put it on the market and was now renting a bland 3-bedroom house on an even blander estate in one of the blandest places on the planet:

Horley. My landlady was BA cabin crew who lived across the road and did nothing but pester me almost every day - it got to the point of me having to hide indoors! Work was going well, I was now on 'auto pilot' and, such was my success, that they asked me to go permanent on a reasonable salary and bonus, which I agreed to. Outside of work my life was pretty pedestrian, I tried to put more time into my girls and my social life (golf and poker) such that it was. I wasn't particularly bothered about a relationship and just got on with life alone.

But by May/June 2008, I felt I needed to do something about being alone. Single life had never really suited me - I don't look after myself properly and go to seed. I signed up to a couple of online dating sites, which was the most bizarre experience, in every respect. I submit a profile, which included all my personal details, a photo, my likes/dislikes and aspirations and I was inundated. Internet dating wasn't mainstream back then and I discovered that as new people registered they attracted a vast amount of attention from others who had been registered for a while, but had either had no success or simply exhausted the current stock. I must have met half a dozen women and found all of them very odd. They all had very strange and different stories and I was both surprised and definitely put off by their fairly 'full on' approach to things. I don't know what I really expected, but it certainly wasn't what I encountered. The meetings were predictably far from natural but it was as if a few words on an internet site precluded the need for the 'getting to know each other' bit. More than once I was invited "back to mine" after just a short meeting over a drink and, despite my 'liberalism', I found that quite distasteful. I gave up being proactive after a few months, the initial surge had gone quiet and so I didn't expect to hear much. But then I was contacted by Chloe, a lady from Reigate, which led to one of the worst experiences of my life!

Chloe seemed totally normal when I met her and even made me think that this internet dating malarkey might be OK after all. She had a son (Josh) and daughter (Ellie) about the same ages as Fran and Steph and had been divorced a few years. Things progressed at a reasonable pace and we got on well. After a while I introduced the children and they seemed to be OK with things too, but I worked out later, when reflecting, that they wouldn't have told me, even if they weren't. That was a pity, but totally understandable given their ages.

Culzean House sold pretty easily – too easily, perhaps. I put it on the market with one agent but within a day or two a friend of another agent knew someone who was looking for a substantial property in one of two roads in Camberley. He called me and after a couple of visits he offered the asking price and the deal was done. The usual formalities followed and shortly after exchange of contracts I received a letter from the original agent (who I had told almost immediately that I had secured a private sale) congratulating me on the sale of the property and enclosing an invoice for nearly £20,000. I was horrified and argued with them that they had nothing to do with the sale, had not introduced the purchaser or participated in any of the sale process. Their argument was based solely on the fact that they had a contract and that the sale could well have been initiated by their board or advertising, neither of which were possible given the speed that things happened. They wouldn't budge and they weren't even prepared to discuss a compromise. I took legal advice and got a fairly ambiguous response like "I might be able to take this on, but there will be costs" and if I were to lose there would also be the legal costs of agents. So, I reluctantly paid and after a few of the expected hiccups the house was sold in August 2008.

I needed to buy somewhere as I couldn't contemplate renting any longer. I was looking around the Reigate/ Dorking area but it was insanely expensive and I was not looking forward to what I might end up with - certainly a huge downgrade from Culzean after splitting the proceeds with Dawn. That provoked a conversation that I wasn't really prepared for. Chloe was also renting, but had a fair sum in savings from her divorce settlement a year or two earlier and just "hadn't got around to buying anywhere". So she offered up a chunk of her money to allow me to buy a better property with the plan that once we had become properly established as a couple then she would move in. If that never happened I could mortgage the house and repay her. The theory was good, I didn't sense any future difficulty (which was somewhat naive) and after several conversations that's what we did. I found a nice house just a short walk from

Reigate town centre, bought it (house number 10) and moved in December 2008. I think it was only a matter of days later, Chloe having been around every day and evening, that I thought the whole thing was just a bit mad and she might as well just move in. No sooner had I suggested it than she did.

So where do I start? Almost immediately, things went downhill. Her demeanour changed and even her children appeared to regard me in a different way. They treated me like a stranger, with very little interaction compared with what went before. I was confused and hoped that maybe it was just the changing environment and that things would settle after a while.

We had been invited on a ski trip in February half term with a group of Chloe's friends and children. Neither of Chloe's children had skied before but she was keen and so we went. I also thought it might be a good way to bond with her children and it would be a fun break for Fran and Steph too ... wrong on every count!

We stayed in a nice hotel in Zermatt and Josh and Ellie were booked in for lessons and went on the first two days. On day 3 they wanted to come out with us and so we mucked around on the green slopes in the morning. Neither Josh or Ellie were particularly competent but Josh wanted something a bit more challenging. I found as easy a blue run as I could and we took a chair lift up. We were coming down very casually and the run was extremely well groomed and well marked at its edges. I had Josh to my right and could see him in the corner of my eye. We rounded a very slight left bend and he failed to turn and went across the piste and over the edge of the run and came off his skis in the powder. I would have laughed had it not been for the scream he let out, I'd be surprised if they didn't hear it in the next village. It simply didn't add up, I saw him clearly cross the edge of the piste, go into the soft powder and fall over. Chloe was hysterical and I was trying to calm both her and Josh, Ellie was screaming too and I think Fran and Steph just stood there staring in disbelief. Worse was to come!

I resisted my desire to drag him to his feet and tell him to 'man up' and tried to patiently encourage him back up and we would get food/drink or such like at the bottom. I was getting nowhere when around the corner came a ski patrol man. He stopped and had a look and tried to move Josh who screamed. He then got on his radio and about 5 minutes later a medic arrived with a ski stretcher, I remember thinking it was getting out of control and I felt embarrassed that we were putting these people out. Worse was to come! When the medic and his colleague tried to get Josh on the stretcher to take him to the bottom of the mountain the intensity of his screams only increased. So the medic said he was calling in a helicopter. I had now had enough and protested with Chloe, I had seen exactly what had happened and she should now put a stop to this absurdity. I was unsuccessful. The helicopter arrived about 10 minutes later and I was told that Josh would be taken to the hospital in the valley and they gave me the details, Chloe went with him. I took their skis and the four of us skied down the mountain to the base station. I wasn't sure what to do but it was lunchtime and I suggested we go into the restaurant area by the train station, get lunch and then we could go the one stop on the train to the next village where the hospital was.

We finished our lunch, got our things together and went out on to the platform. The station was the end of the line and the next train was due in about 5 minutes. The train arrived and as everyone was getting off one of the girls saw Chloe and Josh. Bottom line, no damage done, in fact such was the speed of his miraculous recovery he wanted his ski's so he could go back up the mountain and start skiing again. That didn't happen and led to the most horrendous argument!

The rest of that holiday was a mess and a horrid experience for the girls, but we got through, thankfully on ski holidays there's plenty to occupy. The sting in the tail was that I had put all the travel insurance in my name and I ended up having to pay £500 excess on the £2,200 claim. Frankly I'm surprised the insurance company paid a penny.

Things didn't improve back at home either. I tried to make the peace but it was clear that it wasn't just the ski trip that was getting in the way of things. The children were fine but Chloe's moods were very inconsistent and I never knew what I would encounter. One time I opened my wallet for something and was sure that money was missing, dead sure. I was home alone that day and went and looked in the children's bedrooms, I found nothing but when I went into their bathroom cabinet I found £60 stuffed behind the toothpaste or such like. I wish I hadn't bothered because it caused a huge argument between Chloe and I and I ended up 'the bad guy'.

Then, shortly after, and out of nowhere she accused me of thinking that she was having an affair with her boss. I've no idea what provoked that or why she would have thought so, but she got angrier and angrier until she simply called her boss right in front of me and told him that I thought she was having an affair with him and thrust the phone into my hand so he could tell me he wasn't. All I could do was apologise and said there had been some mix up and I hung up. My immediate thought was that whilst it had never even occurred to me that she might be having an affair with her boss, I hoped she was.

That was the end of course, and I knew I had to somehow unravel myself from this and quickly. Only a matter of days later, that was made very easy for me. One night when I was unable to sleep I went downstairs for a drink and sat at the computer to look at the news or football or such like. When the machine fired up, I was shocked to see an open online chat conversation in what was some sort of sex room. The conversation was graphic and very unpleasant to read. Even worse, as I started to dig around I found more examples. I stayed awake until they were all up and when the kids went off to school I confronted Chloe. I don't know what she said, I don't think I was listening. I told her I wanted out and I was going to get a mortgage to pay her off. Then she dropped another bombshell on me by declaring she wanted her money plus another huge chunk because of the disruption to her life and the distress to her children! I remember vividly, being speechless.

She went off to work, I contacted an estate agent and by the time she returned the house was on the market. Thankfully she packed up and went off to her parents with the kids and I'm not sure I ever saw her again – the only contact I had with her was via solicitors. The house sold pretty easily and, even after just four months, it had made enough to cover all the costs. Unfortunately, though, I took a bath on the division of the house proceeds. I fought it but I had no real appetite for a long, drawn out fight. Chloe was OK, living with her parents or back in rented accommodation but I needed to get away and get a home of my own and put this episode behind me. I soon discovered that being at fault or being a victim makes absolutely no difference in such matters. Nor, to a large extent, does the amount invested by each person have a great deal of bearing, or it didn't appear too. I took a painful financial hit but it was so totally of my own making. I didn't deserve it but I should have been far less impetuous. I got it over with quickly and what I regarded as the worst, short, period in my life was brought to a close with the house sale in July 2009.

Back at work, I had assembled a good team and

refocussed our efforts and there were lots of positives. Andrea went off on maternity leave and I stood in for her on the Executive Committee. One of the senior members was Lesley, the director of travel. She was a likeable down to earth 'Essex girl' who had been at BA for years and she and I got on very well. Before Chloe, she was always encouraging me to find a girlfriend and it was a constant topic of conversation. We were at an off-site meeting one day and, over lunch, she said there was someone at work that would be ideal for me. To a greater or lesser degree I pretty well knew everyone at work and we had fun over lunch with me trying to guess who she was referring to. I eliminated most based on age or marital status and ended up with a list of three: The MD's PA, who was a complete horse nut and who looked very much like a horse too; the mad woman in finance who had been palmed off from department to department and whose only useful contribution was to make tea for anyone and everyone, and then there was Judy in HR. I knew very little about her, but regularly saw her in meeting rooms sat opposite (mostly) crying (mostly) ladies. I had always assumed she was the company 'agony aunt' – someone who you took your problems to and she would be a good listener (she later told me that she did a fair bit of that). Anyway, the conversations with Lesley were fun and although she persisted I didn't take it any further or really seek to understand why she was encouraging me.

After the Chloe episode, I was back to being pretty

miserable. I decided to move back to Camberley where I had good friends and wasn't too far from the children. I found a house, had my offer accepted and tied the purchase date in with the completion date of the Reigate house. In the interim, things were pretty dull so I was pleased when when I got a call from a couple of fellas from Oz that I worked with a few years earlier, saying they were passing through London on the way to Germany one Saturday, and suggested we meet up at Gatwick where they would be staying overnight.

I went into the office that Saturday morning to clear up a few work things, when I got a call from one of them saying that they had to make a last-minute switch and would be heading straight to Germany from Heathrow in the next hour or two. I was really quite disappointed because I was looking forward to seeing them and it would have been a good use of my idle time. It left me a bit redundant and I sat there at my desk wondering what I was going to do with myself.

I don't know why but I pulled up the staff phone directory, found Judy's number and called her, without even really thinking what I was going to say. She answered and I stumbled through something that ended with my asking her if she wanted to meet up for a drink. Somewhat surprisingly she agreed and we arranged to meet on the Sunday night at a country pub. And there started some of the the very best chapters of my life.

17 - LIFE BEGINS (AGAIN) AT 50+

It would be inaccurate to say my life 'began' at 50, because by that time I had already lived two complete lives over, experienced pretty well everything that I could have reasonably expected and accomplished an awful lot. But the way the experience with Chloe ended made me feel like I was, in many ways, starting all over again – especially when it came to relationships. In that respect I had failed - mostly of my making – to the extent that I had resigned myself to the fact that I would never find a long term partner.

My first social meeting with Judy that Sunday night in Lingfield didn't make me feel any different. It was a pleasant evening – we sat in the pub, had a drink or two and chatted about our respective families and a little about our histories. Afterwards, I thought how very nice she was, attractive and with no obvious agenda to push, just a very clearly genuine and decent lady in every respect. Amusingly, at the end of the night, I think we said goodbye and shook hands. I didn't rush to fix up another meeting, I didn't want more disappointment and nor did I want to disappoint. Not seeing her again would be the easy way out, for sure. But it wasn't long before I did ask her out again and I was very happy, even a little surprised again when she accepted. We took things slowly – she had spent the past 10 years bringing up her two boys alone, and she was in no hurry at all to move things along quickly, which was good. Indeed we progressed very slowly, so slow in fact that several weeks passed before we even kissed!

I moved into Beaufront Road, Camberley (house number 11) in July 2009. It was a modest four-bed house, not too far from the town centre and I felt so much more comfortable there than being around Gatwick. Judy came over a couple of times to help organise stuff and lend a hand and my feelings and admiration of her grew, to the point where any thoughts of failure were quickly waning.

Our first date away from a local pub/restaurant was a day at the British Grand Prix. I had been invited by Ladbrokes to a pretty fancy hospitality event and Judy came as my guest. I drove over from Camberley to East Grinstead to collect her then all the way back, and up the M40 to Silverstone. Obviously I did the reverse after the event, which made it a mammoth day out – I left home at 04.00 and got back at nearly midnight. But we had a great time and after I had dropped her home I headed back to Camberley having my first thoughts that we could make a real go of things, I felt comfortable and relaxed around her and I loved her sincerity and total genuine persona. I went back through life to understand what sorts of things might trip me/us up – and had done in the past. I didn't come up with anything and eliminated most of the stuff that had led to issues previously. I did a very through job, there wasn't a hope in hell that I was going to make any more mistakes. But I still wasn't 100% confident by a long stretch.

We had given up shaking hands and had moved on to more conventional affections that a couple show each other, so I took the plunge and invited Judy on holiday to Lake Maggiore in Northern Italy. I had visited a couple of times for work meetings whilst at Prism and it's the most delightful place, somewhere that I knew Judy would enjoy. I wasn't convinced she would accept and I think she had a tough time doing so as she saw it as symbolic of a more serious relationship than where we were at. But she did say yes, we had a wonderful time and from thereon in I think we were firmly together. Any thoughts around my ability to self destruct vanished – temporarily anyway.

Judy is very homely and family-oriented, utterly loyal and trustworthy. Some people at work referred to her as 'Jude the prude', which is unfair, but I understood why. So when I invited her to Las Vegas some weeks after our Lake Maggiore trip, not only was I almost certain that she would politely decline, but if by chance she accepted, then she wouldn't enjoy it. Bigots will simply label it as crass and indulgent and it is if you can't see through the veneer of The Strip and Downtown, but it has so much more to offer and doesn't need a huge amount of imagination to find it. All manner of food can be had and of the highest quality, the hotels are as good as anywhere in the world as is the shopping and there is an endless amount and variety of entertainment, certainly not limited to gambling. It's a place to visit and simply tune out of the realities of life, not that I ever went for that reason, but that's the way it is. But I wanted to see the other sides of Judy and understand as much as I could about her, well that was part of the motive! Somewhat surprisingly, she accepted my invite and we headed there in October 2009. I shouldn't have been concerned, she had a fabulous time doing all the things that you do in Vegas: walked miles and miles; ate and drank too much; shopped; explored and yes, even gambled, I would never doubt again that she knew how to let her hair down and enjoy herself. We both had a ball and I was so happy, as much for her, that she was so comfortable having fun. I knew she was someone that had absolutely everything and I was very fortunate. As it happened, and to my great delight Vegas became a firm favourite for both of us and we were to visit several times and have many happy memories.

Inevitably with things going so well in my personal life things at work went very sour, very quickly. I had been at

Air Miles for over two years had received outstanding appraisals, was regarded as top 5% talent, was one of the senior of the non-director population and had acted as director of the area while Andrea was absent on nine months' maternity leave. But the CEO, Alan Stanwick, wasn't someone who I particularly liked or admired. He had a very high opinion of himself and would frequently convene meetings or kick off initiatives that appeared to be designed to fulfil some sort of personal rather than commercial agenda. That said, he wasn't a man to cross and so I didn't, I was always very respectful of him, which is what he liked. I knew exactly how to behave in the workplace, so life at work was as good as it could be.

Shortly after getting together with Judy, one of our biggest retail clients came to us and told us we needed to drop our price for selling them Air Miles, by 50%. It had recently re-launched its customer loyalty scheme by offering double points to everyone and this meant, for those customers that exchanged points for Airmiles, they would need to buy double the number from us. That was something I don't think they had considered when launching the double points scheme and would immediately add several £'m to their cost base. The account director who looked after the business quickly escalated the matter as we simply couldn't accept that we would have to absorb that kind of cost. I met with my opposite number to try and reason and negotiate. He knew they had made a mistake – most of its customers simply exchanged points for money off at the till so the impact on margin was negligible as it was adjusting prices all the time and was trading price to volume. Anyone who has ever negotiated with this business will tell you, they are notoriously difficult and use their size to dominate any negotiation process but I knew and I believe he knew that we would have to reach a compromise.

Together with my finance people, I spent several weeks working with them to try to find a mutually acceptable middle ground. Eventually we settled on a deal that would see us reduce our price by nearly 20% - so still making a sizeable loss in revenue - but, in return we would get lots of free advertising in their magazine, statement inserts and in-store visibility. The value of the advertising (the price they would charge anyone else) was roughly what we were losing in revenue so, arguably, we suffered no net loss. It wasn't a cost we wanted however, it was of limited value to us, but it was the best I could do. The alternative was that they removed Air Miles from its loyalty program and, not only would we lose a sizeable chunk of revenue, but also a flagship partner. I kept Andrea updated throughout negotiations and, once concluded, I produce the pitch to take to Stanwick.

The meeting with Stanwick was bizarre. Along with the finance team, I had prepared a really robust and compelling pitch. I went through it detailing the history, why we were in the situation and outlining the different stages of negotiations. Stanwick was furious. He screamed at me/us saying that he would not accept this new pricing and to tell them that we would take our business to their main competitor if they didn't back down, before storming out of the room. This was the most absurd suggestion, the competitor was already tied into a multi-year contract with another major loyalty scheme (something Stanwick was more than familiar with). Unsure what to do, I looked at Andrea and she (somewhat) apologised for his behaviour and told us to leave it with her. I assumed it would blow over, a Stanwick 'tantrum' wasn't unusual, although this was a beauty.

It was 'appraisal season' and a couple of days later Andrea casually asked me if I'd received all my 360° feedback. I told her I had and she asked if I had received any from Stanwick. When I said I hadn't heard from him, she thought it might be an idea if I did, so I sent a note and asked him. Boy was I unprepared! Less than 30 minutes later I get a full two pages of the most unreasonable, inaccurate and downright nasty commentary. Completely ignoring all of my work of the previous two years – which had been 'universally' acknowledged, recorded and rewarded – he chose to attack pretty much every aspect of my work, his comments were a work of complete fiction. My instinct was to walk out right there and then, find a lawyer and start a constructive dismissal claim, but two things stopped me. Firstly, Judy and I were doing so well, I knew it was special and I didn't want to prejudice that or cause her difficulty at work. Secondly, the compensation limit for unfair dismissal without racial, sexual or age discrimination was £35,000 and that was nothing like enough. I went to Andrea and she told me to just get on with things and she would talk to Alan. I've seen a lot of stuff in the workplace but I don't ever recall being more furious than I was then. I took the rest of the week off, had I not done so goodness knows what would have happened.

I avoided Stanwick over the next week or two and he did likewise with me. Then Andrea suggested she and I meet in a local pub one evening after work, clearly not a social meeting. Her first words were "This isn't working is it?" "What isn't working?" I responded – and she proceeded to tell me that Stanwick had no confidence in me, that I was a poor negotiator and my high level relationships with our key partners weren't strong enough. Quite how he would even know any of this was a mystery but also – and as Andrea well knew – it was nonsense. But, rather than her telling Stanwick to calm down and behave professionally, she allowed herself to be railroaded by him and I was out on a limb. We talked back and forth but I knew my destiny had been decided and so I waited for the proposition. It came in the form of a sideways move in the business, working for the IT director in a new position called head of business change. I'd have a few project managers and business analysts working for me, but no real remit (well, not at that time anyway) and it was obvious this was a hastily put together idea and one that I assumed they expected me to reject. The alternative was a near six figure pay-off and a few bits and pieces such as keeping some of my benefits for six months, etc. Although I had little intention of accepting the sideways move I needed to think it through.

The timing was dreadful. We were in the middle of a banking crisis and people throughout the financial services industry were being laid off. I was in my mid 50s and so I knew finding a good job was going to be tough and would take time. I had to think it through and I wasn't being given too much time to do so.

I was really disappointed in Andrea. I'd known her for over 20 years and I thought we were close friends and I most certainly hadn't let her down, quite the opposite in fact. She was more than capable of going to Stanwick and telling him to calm down and leave her to manage her function. It didn't require her to fall on her sword and she had more than enough influence over him to put a stop to it. But she didn't. I never understood why and I even asked Burchett what was going on, but he (sensibly on his behalf, maybe) responded by saying: "I don't want to get involved." That really disappointed and surprised me, so much so that I didn't speak to him for more than a decade after that.

I went back and forth with Andrea and the (hugely unimpressive) HR director knowing full well that the new job offer was a smokescreen. They couldn't fire me because of my record, but by taking this new and undefined role they could – and would – be able to find ways to criticise my performance and potentially construct grounds for dismissal down the line. So I was fairly content when they agreed to allow me a six-month probationary period and if, at the end of it, I chose not to continue they would pay me the severance package on the table now. That was the best I could do and for the following six months I did virtually nothing constructive as there wasn't any job to do anyway. The promised project managers never materialised and the analysts I was given were deadwood in the business that had zero influence. But it did give me the time I needed and I spent the vast majority of it meeting headhunters, networking as best I could (not a specialist subject of mine) applying for jobs but getting pretty well nowhere. There were some exceptions, most notably a huge job at NEST as the COO. NEST is ultimately responsible to the DWP and enrols and manages all workers into a workplace pension if a business doesn't have its own scheme. I actually had eight interviews over four months, the last of which was a two-hour presentation to its full board. Apparently I came second!

At the end of those six months, not only had I been unsuccessful in landing a new job, but I had nothing of any interest on the table. I had to make a decision, but there wasn't really anything to consider so I took the severance on offer and quit the business.

It was somewhat satisfying that through this period Stanwick and a very large team had been negotiating with the retail partnership that had so infuriated him and, after several months, had finally signed a contract that was pretty well word for word what I had negotiated and which led to my downfall. I'm not one to say "I told you so" but I took some delight in knowing that I was right all along.

Throughout this period, Judy had been an absolute rock, despite the fact that she could easily have thought it was all too difficult, given her position at work and the inevitable outcome. But I don't think it even crossed her mind. She had met Fran and Steph and got on really well with them; she showed real care for them and they very much liked being around her, we were becoming a family.

I knew my time at BA was coming to an end, so before it did – and I lost my flight benefits – I organised a 10-day holiday for the four of us to South Africa. We flew to Cape Town in February 2010 and then on to Johannesburg where we drove to Kruger Park for a four-day safari. It was a brilliant holiday from the off – we flew there and back in first class and it amused me when we boarded the flight at Heathrow and one of the girls asked me: "What do I do?" Although not the done thing with concession flights, because of my impending departure I replied: "Take everything they offer you," so we all did!

Cape Town was delightful. We stayed in a lovely large apartment in Camps Bay, which was called Panorama 180°, with the most magnificent views. We drove along the coast past the penguins at Boulders Beach, saw some magnificent bays and ate wonderful seafood. We had a great day in Stellenboch and bought a delightful picnic at the Boschendal vineyard. We had another day getting a bit drunk in the V&A waterside area and we also had an adventurous time walking up to the peak of Lions Head, which is opposite Table Mountain, with great views all over Camps Bay to one side and the city to the other.

Our trip to Kruger was adventurous in so many respects, not least the most wonderful opportunity to be up close to the animals in their natural environment. The whole experience completely exceeded my expectations. Other than the wonderful spectacle of the park itself, two rather amusing things stood out. The drive over from Jo'burg is about six hours and we left pretty early in the morning. Once out of the city, the roads were very quiet - apart from when passing through the few areas of population. About an hour from our destination we were driving along at about 110km/h and Judy asked me to slow down a little as we had passed a sign showing an 80km/h limit. I had seen it but couldn't fathom why, given that the road was good, mostly straight and there was no urbanisation at all, nor any traffic to speak of. I think I compromised and reduced to about 95km/h. As we rounded a shallow bend, a policeman emerged in front of me with his arm up, waved me in to the side of the road and asked me to get out of the car. He told me I was doing 94km/h in an 80km/h zone and I immediately acknowledged and accepted the fact that I was speeding. But he was insistent on showing my speed being caught on the camera that his mate had on a tripod on the other side of the road. Despite assuring him that I accepted I was guilty, he insisted and so I walked over to the camera and he showed me a still picture of the car and pointed to the 94km/h number at the bottom of the screen. He then told me that I would have to pay a fine at the nearest police station which was 3km further along the road at a crossroads. He added that I couldn't pay him as he didn't have any receipts. I asked him the procedure and he said he would give me a ticket and to take it to the police station, but that they would only accept cash. I asked him how much the fine was and he said it would be 2,000 Rand (about £100). I told him I didn't think I had that much in cash and he said there was an ATM in a garage next to the police station, but there would be a queue there. I wondered why there would be a queue when we were in the middle of nowhere and hadn't seen a soul for ages. He then repeated that I couldn't pay him as he had no receipts. I then twigged. I asked him if I could pay him if I didn't need a receipt and he said he would have to consult with his colleague. He went across and there was some whispering and he returned and said that would be fine and he would take it to the police station himself. I repeated that I didn't think I had 2,000 Rand and he asked me how much I had. I told him I didn't know as my wallet was in the car and he asked me to go and get it. I went to the car, picked up my wallet and quickly pulled out most of the cash, gave it to Judy and walked back to the policeman, who I now doubted was actually a policeman, despite his shabby policeman shirt and maybe even a sheriff's badge! I opened my wallet and pulled out about 800 Rand and said that was everything I had. He went off to consult with his mate and returned telling me that they would accept this as payment of my fine. I paid and walked back to the car not sure if I was furious or highly amused.

We drove off and actually passed the police station at the crossroads and there was no queue at the ATM! No more than another 2km further on and as I round a bend another policeman jumps out and waves me in. I pull over and wind my window down and before he was able to say anything I tell him that I was driving within the speed limit and I haven't got any money as I gave it all to his friends down the road. He asked me what they looked like and I replied: "I don't know. He was black, wearing a home-made police shirt with a sheriff's badge on it," and then I just drove off. I didn't give it a second thought at the time but, on reflection, it might not have been the wisest thing to do!

Our hotel in the Kruger was a really nice, well set-up lodge. The rooms were laid out in small blocks and between the rooms were fairly large outside areas with walkways connecting the reception, restaurants, bars and the swimming pool. It was right on the edge of a fairly dense bush area and one of the bars was a great vantage point to watch elephants, giraffes and other animals in their natural habitat. One day we were walking back from breakfast when we passed a narrow path that went to a dead end at which there were perhaps a dozen small monkeys, of which some looked like babies. Steph was fascinated and asked me to get a little closer to take some pictures. Naturally I did but as I approached there was an almighty ruckus and I soon had five or six monkeys going for me. I turned and ran as fast as I could, dragging Steph and shouting to Judy and Fran to run. We had no time to think – we all went different ways with monkeys coming at us from all directions. Steph and I ended up in the restaurant but we didn't know where Fran and Judy had gone. I was concerned and went and found Fran on an upper level but below us in an open area that we were overlooking, Judy was being cornered by six monkeys. Other people were now with us and we all started banging the walls and making as much noise as possible. Judy had no exit as she had run down a dead end and it got quite scary. None of us realised just how vicious monkeys could be and thankfully, with all the commotion we were making they backed off. Seemingly the locals carry pepper spray for such incidents, good to know after the event! On reflection those two incidents were amusing but, at the time, each one – for different reasons – were quite harrowing.

It was a wonderful and adventurous holiday and rates amongst the best we've ever done. We got to see all the 'Big 6' and the highpoint I think was the lions. On the morning we saw them our driver headed off and told us we would see the lions today. I wondered how he could be so sure, we were in an area larger than most English counties and I assumed it was a matter of luck. He told me that they had been spotted by another guide but we were so early out (in the dark) I doubted that could be correct. So, I asked him if the lions were chipped and he first replied that they weren't and then he said they actually were but only so they knew where they were when they were sick. I asked him how they might know they were sick but he didn't reply. Maybe they gave them mobile phones?

We rounded off three safaris with an adventure day that included quad biking, zip wire experience and white water kayaking. It's a must do holiday for anyone that hasn't experienced it and we had a wonderful and memorable time.

Before I finally left Air Miles and BA in April 2010, Judy and I took advantage of my concessions one last time and visited Singapore and Penang for 10 days. One of the highlights was having the entire First Class cabin to ourselves on the outward journey, with awesome 360° views of the straights of Singapore on landing. But probably the food in Penang was the most memorable aspect of the trip. We hit Singapore in a horribly humid season, which wasn't ideal and limited our sightseeing but we did manage the obligatory Gin Sling at Raffles. We might not have made the most of Penang, but we ate our way through a vast array of different and delightful cuisines.

Shortly after returning from that amazing trip, I packed up my things, signed the deal and walked out from Air Miles. I was 56 and thought that I might have just done my last days work.

18 - GOLF

I've been through more than my fair share of changes in life – employers, partners, houses – but one (maybe the only?) constant through it all has been something that has consumed a lot of my time (and money!) over the years: golf.

It all started in Bristol when I was in my mid twenties and Andy Pickard got me into the game. I was nervous on my first round at his golf club – so nervous in fact that I refused to tee off on the first tee within sight of the clubhouse, so we started on the second.

When I moved to American Express in the late 1980s, Andy was one of the first people I called to come and work for me. I lived in Brighton and he found a home in Hassocks and we both joined Pyecombe golf club, just under the South Downs, about six miles to the north of Brighton. I became friendly with Burchett and Harty at work, maybe because they were already members, I don't recall. We then became a regular four-ball at the club and that's where we first met Giles, the young assistant professional and who would sometimes join us to play if he was available. When I moved to Avco I even threw some money at him for a couple of years to see if we could help him qualify for the PGA tour. He never made it to the final qualifying school but he gave it a good go. I became a fairly decent golfer. Not as good as the other three, but I got my handicap down to 14 while at Pyecombe, which is pretty steady – not that my game was steady by any means.

In the early 1990s we'd progressed to golf trips. I don't recall why, but we started going to Brittany (and beyond) and it became an annual event with eight players. Early on, there would be the four of us and then we were joined by a couple of semi regulars (Giles and his brother Bobby) and two others who were quite easy to recruit (Chris Fisher, Mike Bowman and others). The routine would be: drive down to Portsmouth; spend a couple of hours in the pub and then get on the overnight ferry to St Malo.

If I had to try and pinpoint the time of my life where I drank and gambled more than at any other time then this was probably it. Our golf competitions were six rounds over four days with the best four rounds counting towards the final aggregate score. It was all very serious and the prize money for the winner and second place was fairly substantial. I am not sure if I was an influencer or influenced, but the idea of an auction was introduced on an early trip. So we'd all put in £100 (or whatever it was) for the first and second place and then an auction would take place, bidding for the players we thought would win the competition. If the player we bought finished in the top three, the person that bought him would win a fairly substantial amount of cash. The only rule was that you could only buy one player. That often meant, after the full round of bidding, one or two players might have one or more winning bids, so some negotiation was required.

Through a process of trial an error, we found that two rounds of bidding was the best way to handle things. So here's the scenario: Tony is the first person up for auction. Harty bids £10, Burchett £20 then Phil £30. It all goes quiet so the hammer goes down and Phil has bought Tony for £30. That process is repeated for all eight golfers and, at the end of the first round, everyone has a price. Then you get the situation where the highest price, let's say Burchett, might be £80 so now Tony might look cheap. The bidding starts again and then maybe Tony gets up to £70, driven by the original low price and maybe two or three who hadn't actually been able to buy anyone yet. Now Burchett looks cheap (it's been said!) so when it gets round to him again, the price starts at £80 and would go to well over £100 – and so it went on. There was so much money sploshing around with the often-ridiculous outcome that the person who bought the eventual winner in the auction would make more than the winner of the actual golf competition! We overcame that by allowing the person who had been bought by another to buy back half of himself, but that gets too difficult to explain! Suffice to say it was all rather extravagant.

If you've been on the overnight ferry to St Malo you'll know they make a bit of an effort to provide 'entertainment'. I'm definitely using that term loosely. By the time we boarded, we would generally have six fairly inebriated men, with the two designated drivers primed and catching up fast with the others. We would sit in the lounge and I vividly recall one year the initial act was a magician. I suspect he had been given a Paul Daniels magic set for Xmas because he was truly awful and I don't think he got a murmur from the audience. That was, until the end, when he announced: "Well, this is it ladies and gents, the last trick of the night." Let's just say he didn't exactly get the response he wanted (or expected, probably!). Up next was an Abba tribute band and I wish I'd kept the pictures. I'm not convinced one of them wasn't the magician with a wig and false beard, while Agnetha was definitely the girl frying the eggs at breakfast the next morning. We weren't even looking at the band but, after a while, one of our group noticed that Harty was missing, he was up on stage in the middle of the four-piece tribute giving his impression of Dancing Queen! He didn't stop there, either and by the end of the set he got rapturous applause from the congregated lorry drivers and caravanner's.

Cards also became a big part of our trips and something I regret. It split the group a little – or sometimes a lot – and it carried on for a few years. I remember one year

Burchett losing every penny he had on the overnight ferry and, by the time we arrived in France, he needed to borrow money to pay his way. Such was the nature of the games that by the time the ship arrived back in Portsmouth, not only had he paid back everything he borrowed but he had more in his pocket than he left home with. Our card playing wasn't clever and thankfully we grew out of it ... eventually.

We went away every year and each time explored a bit more of Brittany and down towards the Loire, then further afield to the west coast around La Rochelle and La Baule. One year we even got as far down as Biarritz on the Spanish border. I could fill another book with funny and memorable stories from golf trips, but here's just a selection:

** It was the last day and so the format had us playing two rounds of golf. At lunchtime Chris Herbert asked Andy if he could borrow his car (a very nice Mercedes) to go back to the hotel and make a call. With lunch over we had about 10 minutes before we were due to tee off, but Chris hadn't returned. We assumed his call had gone on longer than planned, but then the lady from reception rushed in with a look of shock on her face to say that Chris had had a car accident. We asked if he was OK and she said he was and that nobody was hurt but he was about a mile away waiting for a breakdown truck. We had a quick huddle and agreed that as it was the last round and everything to play for then we would continue and sort it out later. The lady was horrified. We finished our round and when we got back to the clubhouse Chris was there. He had forgotten the French drove on the other side of the road and it was a very narrow road back to the hotel. He rounded a bend and hit a Citroën 2CV6 head on, shunting it into a ditch. It was miraculous that nobody was hurt, but the Citroen was totalled and it took about two months for Andy to get his car back.

** Another year we were down past Angers and it was a three-hour drive back to St Malo. There were two ferries a day, one at 08.00 and one at 16.00. We were on the 16.00 and on that day one group of us had a good lie-in, late breakfast and casual drive up. But, in the other car, Andy, Harty and two others decided to play one more round of golf and so they got up early and we arranged to meet them at the port. We arrived at St Malo around 15.00, joined the line and when we started boarding about half and hour later there was no sign of the others. We boarded and went up on deck and watched as the last remaining cars boarded, still no sign. As the ferry was pulling away from the dock we see Andy tearing up the quayside doing about 80 and at one point I thought he might even try to leap across the gap! Those of us on the boat were roaring with laughter as we watched it all unfold.

** In all the years of going on the annual golf trip, I never won one of our 'tournaments'. The nearest I got was in one of the early years and our final round was at a course called St Laurent. We stood on the 18th tee of the last round and I was one point ahead of Giles and Bobby – it was neck and neck (and neck). The hole was straight and over a hill with pine trees lining both sides of the fairway. I hit my ball but sliced it right into the trees but, because it was over the brow of the hill and I couldn't see where it landed, I thought it sensible to hit a second shot (provisional) in case I couldn't find the first. If I didn't, I would use the second ball but that counted as my third shot as there is a penalty shot for losing a ball. Unfortunately I hit my second ball in exactly the same place. There was no point hitting a third ball as that would now count as my fifth shot and way too many to score points on the hole. Giles and Bobby both hit decent drives. When we got over the hill we found both of my balls, one was right in the middle of the fairway and the other in the trees. But then I had a problem. One was a Titelist 1 and the other a Titelist 3 and I couldn't remember which I had hit first and which second. No matter, Giles and Bobby were both reasonable and so I asked them to select, saying that if they chose the ball in the trees as my second then obviously the one on the fairway was my first and vice versa. They had a quick chat and told me that the rules of golf state that if a ball cannot be identified, it cannot be played. Therefore I needed to go back to the tee and play another ball, my fifth shot. I pleaded with them and asked them to be reasonable – we knew these were the two balls I had just hit and they could make the choice. But they wouldn't budge (Blimey! I thought this was meant to be friendly golf with mates!) So I didn't score on the hole and, as it happened, Giles and Bobby scored and we all three ended on the same points. So we had a sudden death play off on the first extra hole and I put my drive in the bunker and that was that. It's a golf story that has haunted me for years!

In the beginning, the golf trips were with an Amex group and then the Avco guys but I also joined another 'tour' with Burchett and Willsy, which they affectionately called BAGS (Big Arse Golf Society). They called it that because they were all, to varying degrees, overweight, which thankfully I wasn't. Here I met up with Gary, Kevin, Finn, Karl and Rory who were all great fun, but professional drinkers and I always struggled to keep up. One trip when we were in Killarney, the kitty ran out of money pretty late at night and we all had to put another £100 in. I had a Guinness and, as it was heading towards midnight, I made my excuses and left. We had to leave next morning at about 06.30 as we had a fairly long drive to Waterville for golf. When I got down into reception the next morning, Finn was asleep on the couch – he hadn't even made it to his room, and as the others all joined us in the lobby, it was clear that they were all suffering the effects of a very long night. We eventually got to Waterville where a full Irish was ordered up by everyone. The bill came and then Burchett asks everyone for another £100 each for the kitty. I reminded them that I put mine in the previous night, just to be told that it had all gone! Goodness knows how, they must have drunk the pub nearly dry and somehow managed to get food at some ridiculous hour in the morning. I protested and we came to a not too satisfactory compromise.

They were a fun group, but difficult to keep up with on most fronts, most of it was instigated by Finn and Rory and involved heavy duty alcohol and food consumption. I remember one amusing conversation when, in all seriousness, one of them suggested that you see very little evidence of overweight elderly people and their conclusion was that after a certain age the metabolism somehow goes to work and the body naturally sheds its weight. They were all intelligent and successful people and I think one or more actually believed it. I looked on speechless.

They played hard and fast. On one trip to the Algarve, the last day's tee pairings and order of play on the first tee was decided by positions in the tournament. So those in positions 5-8 were in the first group and those in positions 1-4 the last group. Within the group, the order for driving off the first tee was in reverse chronological, so the person in eighth drove first, the person in seventh drove second, etc. Somebody came up with a great idea that, as an additional handicap, the person in eighth had to take one big drag on a spliff (Gary had managed to procure some weed) then the person in seventh had to take two big drags and so on until the person in first (Kevin I believe), had to take eight big drags. Fortunately I was in seventh or eighth, so my penalty was fairly moderate. Although, in saying that, I did struggle through holes two, three and four! On top of that, at the halfway house after the ninth hole, there was a refreshment area and Finn (who was in our group) made out that we had all drunk a pint plus a quadruple brandy. So when the second group arrived they had to do the same. We made it look like we had with the remains of booze in glasses but in fact we hadn't drunk anything, but they did. We even hid one of their buggies while they were in the cabin but, even after all of that I still couldn't improve my position and somehow Kevin managed to complete his round and win!

Away from these daft trips I have been so privileged to play some of the best golf courses in the world, courtesy of my work – particularly at Avco/Citi where there was a strong golf culture influenced by the president. The company owned a wonderful golf course in the Rockies (Castle Pines), which we would regularly go to for so-called 'meetings'. But pretty well every management meeting or incentive involved golf and I was fortunate enough to travel far and wide playing a game I loved. I am no connoisseur of golf courses and have tried to identify my favourite one, but it is so difficult. But on my shortlist would be: Turnberry; Desert Mountain; Troon; both Scottsdale (Arizona); Blue Monster at Doral (Miami); La Quinta (Palm Springs) and Torrey Pines (San Diego). A special mention goes to the aforementioned Waterville, too. Closer to home, I really enjoyed St Georges Hill, Walton Heath and Sunningdale.

I played my best golf when living in America. My golf

club, Mission Viejo (known locally as Mission Impossible) was a lovely course and a US Open qualifying course, so by no means easy. I got my handicap down to 12 while I was there, but never managed to hit single figures, which was a lifetime ambition.

My best ever round was a 79 at Pyecombe. I was playing with Giles (the club professional) and coincidentally he also shot a 79. I remember thinking at the time that I had rarely seen Giles play so badly, yet I had just played the round of my life. I guess it put my achievement into perspective.

19 - REGROUP (AGAIN)

I wasn't overly concerned about leaving Air Miles, but I was indignant. The whole sorry episode had put a big dent in my plans, but I thought I could recover quite easily, I always did.

I spent more time with Judy at her home in East Grinstead and I settled into what seemed like endless days of job searching and sporadic networking. I'm hopeless at such things - always have been - and it made me feel quite inadequate. Suffice to say, I didn't get anywhere and the less successful I was, the less effort I put in and the more golf I played.

I was still playing poker and doing quite well - so well, in fact, that I was approached by a staking group. The deal was that they would pay for all my entry fees for poker tournaments and in return I would hand over 50% of any winnings. There were all kinds of responsibilities and measures involved and I would need to check in with a team leader daily. Every second or third day, the team I was in would get together on a video call and spend a considerable time going over winning/losing situations – analysing faults and generally using the collective group to improve our individual games. The staking group had proprietary software that they would load onto my laptop and which tracked every hand I played. My performance would be reviewed by my team leader every week. It was pretty intense and there was a requirement that I play a minimum number of hands daily, which worked out to be about eight hours. I accepted the offer and was moderately successful, in so much as I made enough to pay my way, but I didn't get much pleasure from the whole experience.

One of my poker buddies from back when I started out (Sudsy) was a car dealer and he seemed to be doing well for himself. I thought that buying and selling cars couldn't be difficult so I got together with him and he agreed to help me on my way. He allowed me access to his account at British Car Auctions and I watched a few auctions online – and even put in a few unsuccessful bids. I wasn't too serious, I just wanted to make sure I knew how it worked. When I eventually decided to do something, he asked me how much I thought I could sell a four-year-old Mercedes C-Class estate with a given number of miles on the clock, I gave him a figure. He told me that was about right and that he had one he could let me have for £2,000 less than the figure. This would be my first toe in the water.

I bought the Merc and advertised it in Auto Trader, along with my two-year-old BMW 530 and Judy's eight-year-old MINI. Within a few days the BMW and MINI had sold. I concluded that I had sold them way too cheap because I searched around and realised I couldn't even buy them for that price! The Mercedes, however, didn't sell and I had very few calls, apart from other publications who offered me great rates to advertise with them. One chap did call but wanted to part exchange his 10-year-old Peugeot 405, which I declined. I didn't have a clue how much it was worth and, as we had only the one car, I couldn't imagine using that as our day-to-day transport. I looked to replace the BMW and MINI with two or three cars from auction, but I couldn't get anything at an attractive price. At the same time, Sudsy now told me that the market was difficult and very competitive; bottom line my car dealing career is over pretty much before it started. Not only that, I'd managed to replace our two very nice cars with a pretty crummy Mercedes estate which we go on to keep for another five years.

On the plus side, life with Judy was wonderful. I was living with her in East Grinstead pretty much full time and so was Ian, her youngest son. He is a great boy and was very respectful and gave us our space, which I often felt guilty about. After a few months of living like that, we talked about selling the house in Camberley as it was sat mostly empty and costing money. It was a big commitment for both of us, more so for Judy who had spent the previous 10 years alone raising her boys – and I was not blind to the fact. We didn't act immediately – I think we both sensed there was no hurry so we left things as they were for a while.

Judy had spent quite a bit of time with my girls and I knew Ian very well and John (Judy's other son) less so as he was away from home, but our children had never met each other. I decided to put that right and figured a good way to do that would be to get away somewhere. Given that Barcelona is a fun place it seemed the ideal place for them to get to know each other, so I booked a long weekend in October 2010.

The children actually all met for the first time at Gatwick Airport, when we showed up for the flight. Fortunately, it went incredibly well and they all hit it off immediately, which was a great relief for both Judy and me. The weekend that followed was jam-packed and full of fun – I did it as spectacularly as I could. We toured the entire city and did the Blue and Red hop-on, hop-off bus routes (a must for anyone visiting Barcelona) and walked extensively. We visited one of my favourite restaurants (The Four Cats) and we drank to (mild) excess. On the second night, we ended up in a pavement cafe and I taught them all how to play 'To my left, to my right', a pretty lethal drinking game, and they got the hang of it very quickly and thoroughly enjoyed themselves. I still have a vivid picture of Fran drinking pints like a professional. Judy and I couldn't keep up for the entire night and Fran and John also headed back to the hotel 'early'. Meanwhile, Ian and Steph decided to go down to the marina area to find some late night action. Before they left us, Judy gave Ian a lecture about how he was to look after Steph!

We all met up the next morning, Steph was in one piece, apart from a mild hangover. Ian, however, had seemingly been mugged and had his wallet taken. I say seemingly because he wasn't 100% sure – he said he could have just lost it or even given it to someone! But it did cause some smiles. Fran was particularly hungover and we spent the last morning of our trip gently strolling Las Ramblas and the surrounding area. We were in Pull&Bear when Fran called me – she was upstairs and I was downstairs – telling me she felt dreadful. I told her I would be up and when I got there I learnt from Steph that she had just been sick on her phone, but had made it into the store's toilets. When she came out she looked the worse for wear but had also washed her phone off under the tap not thinking that it wasn't water resistant. Fran had a real knack for losing, eating or just destroying her phones – generally just when she'd started a new two-year contract.

Barcelona was not only fun and a success in terms of introducing the children to each other, but it gave Judy and I the confidence to move forward with our plans for each other. I don't know why, but we called the trip 'Fam a Lam' and then 'Fam a Lam 1' as I fully expected there to be more.

Around this time, we applied to become season ticket holders at Brighton & Hove Albion, who were moving into a wonderful new stadium the following season (2011/12). I had been an avid fan of *The Albion* since the early 1970s, when I used to regularly attend games at the old Goldstone Ground, courtesy of Mrs Bostock and her generosity. For the most part, the team languished in the bottom two leagues but, in 1978, they were promoted to the first division and managed to stay up for three seasons. During that time, my favourite player was Michael Robinson, a very handy centre forward that we bought from Manchester City and sold to Liverpool when we were later relegated. Sadly, he died a few years ago of cancer.

Back in the 1970s and 1980s, a top-class footballer would retire in their mid 30's and buy a pub or a small business. Sky TV changed all of that in 1992 with the arrival of the Premier League and TV rights deals worth millions of pounds to clubs in the league. Having seen what football – and footballers – used to be like, I absolutely loathe much about the modern game, including the finances. That footballers can make such obscene amounts of money (at the time of writing, Ronaldo has just signed for Al Nassr – a Saudi Arabian team very few fans outside Saudi would've heard of – and is being paid more than £3m a week) is borderline criminal. I live in hope that, somehow, it will all come crashing down and we can get back to good, honest genuine sport, but it will never happen. I do feel something of a hypocrite, attending lots of football games, but I vehemently refuse to subscribe to Sky Sports, which is the cause of the madness and that's about the only stand I can make. Regardless of the obscenities of money such is the passion for 'my' football team I am definitely being buried with my blue and white scarf.

We also 'branched out' and started to take in a few away games a season and visited such salubrious grounds as Bristol City, Millwall, Charlton, Nottingham Forest, Ipswich and Norwich – and many more. The biggest away day was undoubtedly the 2019 FA Cup semi final vs Manchester City. Kick off was at 17.30 and, even though we got an early train at 10.00, it was standing room only. When we got to London it looked like the entire West End was full of Brighton supporters. We ended up around Baker Street and couldn't find a pub that wasn't overflowing with Brighton fans – it was very much a party atmosphere. We lost the game 1-0 and were never really in it, but the experience was fabulous. I think we might have done a deal with Manchester City beforehand, if we didn't make any attempt to score then they could score one and stop there. It was as one sided a 1-0 as you'd see but we weren't humiliated.

Before we got our season tickets, Judy hadn't been to more than a couple of games in her life but, as is her way, she became hugely committed to it. She knows all the words to all the songs and seeing her enjoying herself the way she did made me smile. Ask her "What's the referee?", for example and she'll give you the 'right' answer! We had great seats and made a few football friends both at the stadium and at the Horsham supporters club who got together regularly. The Horsham group would get all sorts of players, ex-players, managers and even the Chairman come along and give us updates and insights. We also had friends that would come along, regularly or occasionally and so football was a reasonably good social opportunity for us too. It's a pity I didn't get to see us play in Europe - I think I might have only missed it by a year or two, such is the progress at the club.

I can't talk about 'my' football team without mentioning Tony Bloom. There are a few people I have admired through my life and he is certainly one of them. Tony (along with the wonderful Dick Knight and numerous determined supporters) literally saved our club from certain extinction when we were homeless, broke and languishing at the very bottom of the football league. There are many books written on that period and perhaps I shouldn't single one out but 'Build a Bonfire' by Stephen North and Paul Hodson, really is a very good read, whether you are a fan or not. Anyhow, Tony Bloom, entrepreneur and very handy and well known poker player, is a lifelong supporter of the club and became the owner in 2009. He immediately invested (if there is such a thing in football) c£100M of his own money, facilitating the move from a run down converted running track to a wonderful new 30,000+ stadium which had been planned, but funding was far from guaranteed. He has since made further substantial investments which, amongst other things, have allowed for the development of truly world class training facilities. The successes the club have achieved these past few years are absolutely down to his commitment and leadership. I've been fortunate to meet him a couple of times - unfortunately I missed him at the poker tables - and he is a remarkably humble man, choosing to travel to many away games on the train and mingle with fans, as well as occasionally turning his back on the Directors box and joining the fans in the away end. He not only has my admiration but great thanks for his contribution to the success of 'my' club.

In the spring of 2011 I put my house up for sale and it sold without too much difficulty. I moved in with Judy and my belongings were either stored in her garage or used to replace some of her things. We contemplated my living in her house on a permanent basis, but concluded it wasn't the right move. Not only was it quite a small home but it was 'hers' and we both thought it best to start afresh and have something that was 'ours', so we put her house on the market.

I was happy to stay in East Grinstead, but Judy wanted to leave the area and we decided to look in Horsham. It was a nice town, with good road and rail links and midway between her work at Gatwick and the girls in Cranleigh. We got a decent offer on her house fairly quickly, which we accepted but, unlike mine, the sale wasn't straightforward and the buyers mucked us around a lot. We started looking for property and I was much more inclined to go for a higher-priced house, as I was still convinced I would get a job. After nearly a year of looking for one, it was clearly more to do with pride than reality. Thankfully Judy was more realistic and persuaded me to be less ambitious.

We found a lovely house in Horsham, a short walk from the town centre and put in an offer which was accepted. There were, however, several hurdles put in our way over the next few months. Firstly, Judy's buyer let us down on dates numerous times, which meant we needed to shift things around on our purchase. Eventually, the people we were buying from issued an ultimatum that we either exchange by a certain date or they would put it back on the market. We went ahead and exchanged on the 'absolute total assurance' given by Judy's buyers that they would exchange a few days later and complete on the same date as had been set for the Horsham purchase. I knew it was a risk but we had little choice. Unsurprisingly, the buyers let us down yet again and we had a highly stressful couple of weeks liquidating every asset we could lay our hands on in order to complete the purchase, but we got there. Three weeks after that, we eventually completed the sale of Judy's house.

20 - JUSTICE

We moved into Coolhurst Lane in July 2011 (12th house owned) and were delighted with our decision to relocate to Horsham. The only downside was that the rear of the house – where the kitchen, dining area and study were located – faced North, which meant the areas we occupied most during daylight hours didn't get much light – and no sun. Suffice to say it was the first – and last – time I'd lived in a house with that aspect. The only saving grace was that house had a long garden and the patio at the bottom got plenty of light and sun.

We quickly settled into the house, but also made some improvements. Out went the old kitchen and down came the wall between it and the dining room, creating a large kitchen-diner. To be honest, there wasn't that much else to do and the place served us well. Set in a small cul-de-sac, it was very quiet and all the neighbours were very friendly, we never had any neighbour issues whatsoever.

On the work front, I had all but given up looking for a job and spent most of my time playing poker for the staking business.

Such was our settled situation that 2012 was a pretty uneventful year, the highlight probably being called up for jury service. I attended the Crown Court in Brighton and was directed to a large waiting room with all the other new jurors for that week. A court clerk entered and called out 14 names and we were taken into another room. There we met the senior clerk and were told the case that we would be hearing – it was a rape case. We are given a few more general details, such as times of the sessions, how long the trial is expected to last (which, in this case, was two weeks) and how to claim our expenses. All the potential jurors were asked about their availability, any conflicts and then 12 were selected – as basic as names in a hat. Just before 11.00 we entered the courtroom and so began what was a most harrowing fortnight – and an experience that I wouldn't wish on anyone.

The judge introduced himself, told us what role he played and then took us through the process. He explained our responsibilities and the need for strict confidentiality – we weren't even supposed to talk about it with our partners. He also told us that in considering all the evidence presented, we should always keep in mind that in order for us to find the accused guilty, we must believe it to be 'beyond reasonable doubt'. The accused was then brought into the dock and the respective legal counsels took us through their opening comments, which was basically a high-level summary of the position of the victim and defendant.

The victim was an 18-year-old girl from a town to the north of Brighton and who had been experiencing difficulties at home with her single mother and a string of boyfriends (of the mother, not the victim, that is). She was clearly neglected and admitted to being a heavy drinker. She also claimed to be a virgin prior to to the night in question. On that night she said she had drunk over three quarters of a bottle of vodka at home, before going for a walk. She passed the railway station where she bumped into the defendant, who was buying a burger at a van outside. She said she asked him for a bite of his burger and then they walked together towards the town centre when he suggested they walk down an unlit pathway through the woods for a kiss and a cuddle. She agreed but, instead of a kiss and cuddle, he raped her. She then stumbled out to the roadside where she was seen by a couple driving past who had to swerve to avoid her. The couple then took her straight to a police station.

The defendant claimed he was standing at the burger van when he was approached by the girl, who asked for a bite of his burger. She then asked where he was going and he said he was going back to his room in town. She suggested she walked with him and when they got to the pathway she asked him if he wanted to go down for a kiss and cuddle. He didn't deny he had sex with her, but claimed it consensual. He said he had no idea she was drunk and didn't believe she was. He said it was over very quickly, he went one way, she the other and she gave no indication of being distressed.

There was little evidence to support either account. The people who picked her up from the roadside gave statements in court and confirmed she was stumbling by the roadside and was distressed. We saw CCTV of her at various points and one thing that struck me was that she didn't look like a drunk person walking, she appeared to be walking with more purpose. When she got to the train station, she disappeared into a doorway and when she reappeared a minute or two later she was staggering. It was odd and one of the two or three things that I kept coming back to.

We heard character statements from both sides. He was Polish and I was stunned to hear his reply to the question "Where have you been since you were arrested 11 months ago?" "In the sex offenders unit at Lewes Prison"," he answered. For 11 months! He came across as a decent young man (as best one can tell, but certainly respectful to the process) and had no criminal record, or not that we were made aware of. I tried not to let that influence me but, at least, he didn't fit what I found myself imagining as a stereotype rapist. I tried to banish those thoughts too.

When the young girl was brought in to give her evidence - and suffer the ordeal of cross examination - a curtain was placed between her and the accused and the viewing gallery. She was obviously very distressed and it was tough on her. There were numerous pauses during which she had to compose herself. One thing that struck me during this part of proceedings was that there was nobody in the public gallery for her. I don't really know what I expected, certainly her mother, maybe some friends and relatives – even a social worker – but the only people there were the two or three reporters that had been present throughout.

After nine days, the judge summarised the case for us, highlighting all the critical points that he had noted. He reminded us of our obligations and then we were taken to a room adjoining the courtroom to come up with a verdict. This was on the Thursday of the second week and about an hour before lunch. We elected a spokesperson (not me, thankfully) and we debated all the evidence and our thoughts on each aspect of the evidence. We had flip charts and white boards and the debate was healthy and good ideas were surfaced and discussed. After a couple of hours, we agreed to go around the table and get everyone's view: guilty or not guilty. About half way around, a young man who had contributed nothing to that point was asked and his reply was "Well, it doesn't matter what we think the judge obviously thinks he's guilty." I didn't know whether to laugh or cry – it was clear he had no idea and, indeed, showed little interest. I doubt I was the only one that wanted to kick him. That first round of voting had us split equally: six guilty and six not guilty. The clerk of the court would come in every hour or so to ask if we had reached a verdict. We hadn't and each time we voted after a period of discussion it ranged from seven guilty and five not guilty, to three guilty and nine not guilty. We were back in on the Friday and the same was happening. I was beginning to think that there might need to be a retrial, or the judge might agree a majority verdict.

I was fairly consistent in which way I was going and that was not guilty. I really did struggle with it though - I wasn't at all sure but I was constantly aware of the emphasis the judge placed on 'beyond reasonable doubt'. I couldn't get that out of my head. I hated every minute of the trial and having to reach a verdict - I wanted the ground to swallow me up and release me from this obligation. For probably the only time in my life, I felt totally incapable, which was rotten, given the stakes were so high.

I believe the British justice system is trumpeted as one of the best in the world. However, on the evidence of my experience, it most certainly isn't - not by a long way. Or, if it is one of the best in the world, goodness knows how bad it is elsewhere.

1. We still couldn't get a unanimous decision by mid-afternoon on Friday and the clerk of the court came in and told us we would need to return on Monday morning if weren't able to reach a verdict in the next hour. At that point, we were 9:3 in favour of not guilty. Once the clerk

had left the room, the three holding out for guilty were all among the majority who immediately focussed on having to come back on Monday. Within a few minutes, we had our unanimous decision of not guilty! Words failed me – I even contemplated changing my vote to guilty in order to force the issue. On reflection, I wish I had. The fact is that the young man walked free because jurors didn't want to come back the following week.

2. We reconvened in the courtroom where the judge asked us for the verdict, which the spokesperson gave. He then immediately instructed the accused to be released and who then simply walked out of the courtroom, out of the building and into central Brighton. Having been in prison for 11 months I don't believe he had anywhere to go and probably no money. Despite being found not guilty and released, I felt some pity for him. A few of the jurors who came by train met up at a bar in the station to have a beer and say goodbyes. Several of us were still concerned that we might have got the verdict wrong. I know I purposely avoided any local news for many weeks following the trial, fearing I might see his name in a report of being arrested for rape. I didn't sleep well at all for an awfully long time – the whole experience haunted me.

3. Maybe more harrowing for me was that we weren't asked for any explanation or logic as to how we arrived at our decision. Maybe not for the courtroom, but I had some expectation that a court official would sit us down afterwards and allow us to explain. Not a thing. We

simply walked away. Who knows how the information was conveyed to the young lady? Nobody knew why we had found him not guilty and nobody appeared remotely interested. Another reason I avoided local news and couldn't sleep was that I didn't want to read anything about her, goodness knows how she would react. I felt so guilty that she didn't have any explanation whatsoever and I believe that to be totally wrong.

So, all in all, I can confidently say that serving as a juror was one of the most unpleasant and upsetting experiences of my life. Thankfully it's only an exercise that (generally) comes round once in a lifetime.

The other event of note in 2012 was that I heard from Dave Fretter again. He called me out of the blue after nearly 20 years. I think he even apologised for his behaviour after I got him a job – was fired and just left with no word – but I understood. I asked him how things were, fully expecting to hear a pretty grim account and, unsurprisingly, that's how it started. His friend Alec had got him a job at the Halifax, which had started well but there was a falling out somewhere down the line and Dave was fired. He ended up living with his Mum and was in a pretty dire way when he got a call from someone he had worked with at Churchill Insurance, asking if he were interested in joining with six others who were starting a new insurance business. He had to commit a decent amount of money (£40,000 as I recall) and he did so, although I'm not entirely sure where he got it from. His job was to set up and manage the call centre – not even

HE could get fired from that! It all went well and he was pretty much left alone to run things himself. About five years later, the business was approached by AXA, who bought it for a sum that made Dave several millions of pounds! The story was incredible and I was so happy for him – I regarded him as a lottery winner.

21 - WEDDING DAYS

In February 2013, Judy was desperate to get away somewhere warm and sunny. The previous February we had gone down to the Spanish coast between Valencia and Alicante, which was lovely but fairly cool during the day and downright cold at night. We actually went there with half an idea that we might buy a home to escape to in winter. But we soon ruled that out given the low evening/night-time temperatures. So this time she suggested Tenerife. I knew nothing about the Canary Islands and, truth be told, wasn't even really sure where they were. But I agreed because it was a relatively short flight and Judy thought it would be warmer than mainland Spain. We were good friends with Stewart, who worked with me at Avco, and Ellen and so we invited them along. We had a great week by the sea in the south west of the island, near Los Gigantes. The daytime temperatures were about 25° and nights no lower than 16 or 17°. We talked again, as people often do on holiday, about maybe buying somewhere and even looked in estate agents windows, but did no more. I can't say I was completely sold on the idea, plus it would mean parting with a big chunk of our savings. We came home and that was that – or so we thought.

Soon after getting back from Tenerife I (clumsily) proposed to Judy. I was absolutely certain she was right for me and hoped that I would be right for her. She accepted and, when discussing wedding plans, was of a similar view to me. We should go away somewhere, just the two of us and get married quietly and then announce it to our children and families when we got back. Neither of us felt comfortable making too much of a spectacle of it. We settled on Las Vegas – we both liked being there and, after doing some research, discovered that there were quite normal weddings on offer and not all of them were drive-throughs or involved an Elvis impersonator. In June 2013, we headed off only telling the children of our plans a few days before flying out. We were both thrilled that they all gave us their blessing.

We had already booked the wedding venue and before the big day, we headed downtown to the civic centre to get our licence. As we were near to the venue, I suggested we walk there, have a look and make sure everything was set for us. As we turned the corner into the street where the venue was I was surprised to see a quite magnificent church, I wasn't prepared for that at all and it felt almost intimidating. I shouldn't have worried – as we got to the front of the church I realised it was just a standard, rectangular three-storey office building with a vinyl-like church front stuck onto it. Only in Las Vegas!

We married two days later, Judy was stunning in a light blue dress – I was as proud as punch. Believe it or not, our service was both charming and emotionally heart warming. I struggled to maintain composure and it was – and is – one of the happiest days of my life. I think the fact that it was just the two of us made it more meaningful; we had no other distractions. We had a limo that took us to one of our favourite restaurants – Roy's – and they looked after us so well. It was a day I'll never forget and also one I think about often.

We returned home and took our children and Judy's mum, brother and sister to lunch at the nearby South Lodge hotel which finished off our celebrations well.

The next time we went to Tenerife was in February 2014, for another fix of winter sun, this time heading out with Dave Fretter and his partner Barbara. We returned to the same apartments we'd stayed in the year before, just outside of Los Gigantes. I learned more about Dave and his new-found wealth. We had already visited him the previous summer. I remember thinking I was proud to have owned a house with just a name and no number - well Dave's house was just a name and not only did it not have a house number, it didn't even have a street name. It was just the name of the house followed by the name of the village.

Dave didn't know too much about Tenerife either and he was also taken by the wonderful weather and the area. Around the apartments was a dramatic landscape and oodles of nice cafés, bars and restaurants. One day we were walking along the coastal path and passed a lovely residential community. Over their perimeter wall we could see large, well tended gardens, a huge pool and solarium area, alongside very nice traditionally looking Spanish-style houses. Dave was clearly admiring them and remarked that it must be nice to live there. We only walked about another 20 or 30 feet when we saw a house inside with a 'For Sale' sign on it. I told him to give them a call but he wouldn't, so I did. It was a private sale and I arranged with the owner for us to go and see it the following morning. We did but it was only one bedroom and Dave said he would need two at least. But we took the opportunity to walk around the community and it was gorgeous. There were 36 houses spread over a very large area and in quite stunning gardens. It was gated and very secure, ideal for leaving for long periods. It was directly adjacent to the sea looking towards the island of La Gomera, south-west facing so had sun from dawn till dusk and the perfect location for some spectacular sunsets. Dave was smitten and the next day we visited an agent who had two properties for sale in there and which we visited immediately. By the end of the week, he had paid a 10% deposit on a three-bed house in the pool area of the community. I felt chuffed for him and was glad that I encouraged him. I've never believed in 'I need to think about it', if there's stuff to think about then think and make a decision. JDI (Just Do It) is a core philosophy I have carried through life, to my detriment only very occasionally, but mostly it has served me very well indeed.

By mid-2014 I was not only tiring of poker but I needed something more stimulating to occupy my time. As something of a last resort I decided to write a short 'sales pitch' for Tony Cooper and hand-deliver it to all the large employers in Horsham. What I didn't really appreciate was that there weren't any large employers in Horsham – apart from a pharmaceutical business (no good for me), the County Council (goodness, no!) and maybe three others. So I was fishing in a very small pond. I eventually identified four businesses, did a little research and tailored my approach. I was surprised and delighted to get a response from two of them. One was a charitable housing association but, after meeting with them I decided it really wasn't for me, and the other was an IFA (Independent Financial Advisor) that had branched out into technology. It provided other IFA's up and down the country with a back office system that would pull all their clients' equity investments (Pensions, ISAs and general investments), wherever they might be, into one single view.

I met with them and they liked my varied background and experience and asked me to join them on a freelance basis to create and manage a robust prioritisation process for their IT development. They admitted it was in something of a mess and had huge backlogs, I was more than willing to get stuck in. The day rate wasn't brilliant, but they seemed decent people and it definitely wouldn't be a pressurised job – plus I could walk to work in 10 minutes. The first thing I did when I got back home was to Google 'World Class Systems Prioritisation' and, by the end of the next day, I had a solution and all the information I needed to implement it.

I started work the following week. It felt great to be able to walk to work, the company had given me six weeks to come up with the plan and I soon found I had absolutely nothing to do! I spent a few days putting together a very McKinsey-like pitch but, after that, I was really scratching round for things to do. It was an open plan office and I had nowhere to hide – indeed my desk was adjacent to a busy walkway, so pouring over North Stand Chat (the Brighton and Hove Albion football forum) or playing poker wasn't feasible. I somehow managed to occupy my time and eventually presented my pitch to the management team, who unanimously accepted it. We set up the priority meetings every two weeks, which gave me something to do one day every two weeks but, in the interim, I was mostly redundant.

I was gaining a good understanding of the business and, to accelerate my knowledge, my boss decided I should sit next to one of the most knowledgeable people in the office, who delivered training to newly recruited IFA firms. Sophie was a very likeable and chatty young lady, a couple of years older than Fran and I hit it off with her immediately. We have stayed in touch ever since and we often meet with her and her now husband Craig. Sophie began trying to teach me the intricacies of the systems but I wasn't really that interested and so we spent most of the time just chatting about stuff. She was friends with the daughter of one of our neighbours so that got some airing and she was having difficulty with her landlord, which was also interesting and allowed me to get my teeth into something and advise her how to tackle it. I also tried to recruit her to become a fan of Brighton & Hove Albion, but never succeeded there.

My prioritisation meetings were something of a disaster. There was little, if any, governance in the business – at least as far as IT was concerned. And although we now had a robust process, almost everyone ignored it, especially the senior people. I could see this was likely to put me at risk so, after four months of struggle, I suggested to my boss that I could be more productive in other ways and, as the process was now bedded in, I could hand it over to someone else. It wasn't at all credible or convincing, but it was the best I could come up with! Surprisingly, he bought it and I was free of the responsibility.

I now had to invent a new job for myself. There were recurring issues that firms had getting access to some, or all, of their clients' investments and generally it was because they had keyed something incorrectly or their security details weren't set up properly. Those errors did cause a lot of headaches, though, so when I suggested I could fix them, the business was delighted. What it didn't really appreciate – and nor did I at the time – was that the fix was generally so simple it could be done in a flash and, by doing it properly (something they had never done), it could be fixed permanently. I was a huge success and they soon regarded me as the font of all knowledge when it came to investment valuations. Therefore, I found it easy to account for my day.

Sophie was still sat next to me and, by now, I understood that she didn't really enjoy her work and she was paid little more than minimum wage after nearly five years. She was brilliant too and the business massively undervalued her. So I spoke with Judy and a couple of the guys at Air Miles and got her an interview, which she sailed through. She quit the business and I was thrilled for her, but I also had to reassure my boss that her joining the business I had left a year or so earlier was a pure coincidence. For the record, I apologise for that – but it's how the business world operates.

Sophie has gone from strength to strength and deserved it. She moved from Air Miles after about three years to Amex (and I take a little credit for that, too!) where she is today, doing very well. She and Craig eventually married at the third attempt – Covid had been responsible for the cancellation of the previous two attempts. They have made a nice home in Horsham and we see them fairly often. When they were planning their wedding, I suggested they get their wine from a fantastic warehouse in Calais. It's a huge place with literally hundreds of wines and, because the French tax their wine at such a low rate, the prices were a fraction of what they were at home. Sophie and Craig liked the idea and we agreed to go with them as we could use a top-up of wine ourselves, plus we knew how it worked. It was a fun day. We went over on an early Eurotunnel and the warehouse was only a ten-minute drive the other end. By about 11.00 we were in the enormous tasting room and by lunchtime Sophie was completely pissed (sorry, Sophie) – it was so funny. But we accomplished our mission and they returned with about 200 bottles of wine all ready for their wedding the following May... which was cancelled. So they rearranged it to the following May... which was also cancelled. Finally – and with Covid on the run – they managed to actually have their wedding the following June. By which time, they had drunk all the wine they had brought back from France!

Back to work and, in 2015, I had a problem. With Sophie gone, there was nowhere for me to hide. I was being paid for 37.5 hours a week and I estimated that I was doing about 10 hours of actual work. I wanted more, but I could never pin down my boss, who worked remotely, to actually give me anything to do. I knew it was unsustainable. At that time, the business was growing rapidly and both desk space and car parking was becoming an issue and I saw my opportunity. I suggested to my boss that I work from home and that I could clear my workload in three days (or 22.5 hours) a week, so it would save them space and money. I also proposed they increase my day rate by 30%, but there was still a marginal cost benefit. I knew them well enough by now not to be surprised when they agreed. Yes, I would do my job and do it well, but I could perform it leisurely and I would have total freedom. It really wasn't like work at all.

22 - TENERIFE

Dave and Barbara went over to Tenerife in the early part of summer in 2015 to complete the purchase of their house – and we had several calls while they were there just hearing all about it. During one call, Dave floated the idea of us buying a house there too. He told us there were two other houses for sale in the community and we would really like it there and it would be good for them to have someone nearby. I immediately dismissed the idea, not only had I still not got my head around spending extended periods of time away and in the same place, but I didn't really want to part with £250,000 that might be needed for other things.

Dave persisted over the coming days and even, very generously, offered to buy 50% of the house himself, which now made the thought much more attractive, of course. Judy and I chewed it over and over and eventually (days later) agreed that we would go for it. We knew the community from our previous visits and we had even seen the house that Dave was suggesting. Over the following days, we put in ever-increasing offers, but the owner was holding out for a price that I thought was unrealistic so I thought that was that. Then Dave called, telling me another had just come on the market – the owner wanted a quick sale due to illness and it was one of the largest on the development on the edge of the garden area, with almost complete privacy. Fast forward five days and we had signed contracts for a lovely three-bedroom house, with two large outdoor terraces and lovely views. The only slight problem was that we hadn't actually seen it!

In September 2015 we travelled to Tenerife, signed the contracts and took ownership. The house was fully furnished, but we spent the first few weeks making several trips to charity shops and second-hand furniture shops to dispose of a lot of stuff. It was exciting, shopping for nearly a houseful of furnishings in one go and by the end of October we had it set up the way we wanted.

We also wanted to do more substantial improvements and we knocked through one bathroom into a small cupboard type room to make a much larger bathroom with a walk-in shower. We also replaced the kitchen entirely and later we replaced every wooden framed external window and door with double glazed aluminium (UPVC doesn't work there due to the intensity of the sun). All of these improvements left us in a bit of a tricky position with Dave. He had bought 50% of the property and here we were spending a considerable amount improving it and, therefore, increasing the value. It was a difficult discussion but, thankfully, one that he acknowledged and we came to an agreement which suited both of us.

It didn't take long at all to gravitate from reluctant buyers to realising we had done one of the best things in our life together. Tenerife became a true home from home and, with lots of other British people in similar positions, we enjoyed a good social life. Unsurprisingly, we saw a lot of our friends from home who took the opportunity to visit us during the long winter months.

The village/town where we lived had more than enough going on and we were active in every respect. I got our TV set up courtesy of the wonderful Firestick (cough) and we quickly settled in to five-month stays from the end of October until mid-March, with just a two-week break to come home over Christmas. Having endured the last two winters back here in the UK, I struggle to understand why anyone who has the capability to get way doesn't do so.

It wasn't long after settling into Tenerife that I took on the role of president of the community. I was voted in unanimously, largely because nobody else wanted to do it. In the past they even had situations where nobody would put themselves forward, so they did the only democratic thing and pulled a name out of a hat. When

Brenda, a 93-year-old widow had her name pulled out it was a sure sign that things would go downhill rapidly.

With all due respect to the previous incumbents, the management of the place was shocking. The responsibility for work was outsourced to a management company who were, quite frankly, taking the piss. There was no financial control, service fees were increasing needlessly and when you looked hard at the place it was just a bit tired and tatty in places, with a fair amount of rotten infrastructure. On top of that, there were no reserves (money for urgent works) and any time anything out of the ordinary needed doing – such as a new heat pump for the swimming pool – all the owners had to cough up a share of the cost.

I got really stuck in. I wanted to immediately fire the management company, but I would need the owners to support me in a vote. I knew the lady who ran the company had numerous long-term friends as owners, so that was going to be difficult. So I just had to beat on them – and beat on them I did. I didn't given them a minute's respite and although it consumed a huge amount of my time I kept on them and slowly prevailed. It was highly satisfying to be able to make progress and many residents later told me it was the first time in years they had seen real improvement in the management of the community.

I completely changed the way the management company delivered our services and, rather than go out to tender for every tiny little job, I had us employ the equivalent of 1.5 of our own 'handymen'. They were then able to: tend to our four acres of gardens; maintain and clean our huge pool; keep all the common areas clean and tidy and do all the much – and frequently – needed painting, plastering and ad hoc repair work. It saved us a small fortune. I changed so many things that after three years, it was managed completely differently.

I was president for five years before having to stand down due to my illness and the need to sell up. But, in that time, I had put a stop to the increasing fees and began reducing them. I also accumulated nearly €50,000 in our reserves as well as making numerous improvements. The place looked and felt so much better. Sadly, knowing what I do now, it will deteriorate quickly and the management company will get straight back to fleecing the unsuspecting owners. Oh well – all I can say is that I did my best.

Being in Tenerife could have been problematic from a work perspective but I had an IP phone which the business gave me to work at home with and it was simply a case of unplugging it and plugging it back in when I got to Tenerife. To all intents and purposes I was still sitting in Horsham, indeed they thought I was. It was fabulous I would do my 3 days a week sat out on our upper terrace, taking in the sun and feet up. After a couple of years I even told them what I was doing, sought their approval which they willingly gave. But the biggest plus was being away from the horrid British weather, life couldn't get much better. Unfortunately, the events of 23rd June 2016 were to cause a seismic shift in our plans for our time spent abroad.

Who likes politics or politicians? Even today, many years later, I have no idea why David Cameron decided we should have a referendum to determine if we should stay in the European Union. I don't recall anything other than the usual anti-Europe rumblings that had persisted for years by a small, but vocal, minority of implausible and irrelevant characters. We were (as a country) doing OK – certainly no worse than others – and there simply wasn't any reason to ask people that don't have a clue to decide if we should stay in the EU.

I've been ashamed of a few things and not voting in the referendum is one of them. In my defence, we were in Tenerife at the time but I know I could have found out how to register for a postal vote (even though the postal system in Tenerife barely works), but I guess it was just laziness. Also, I couldn't even contemplate the British public voting to leave. It was as unlikely as Turkeys voting for Christmas, so there really wasn't any importance for me to find a way to vote. I've already spoken about what I would do if I ruled the world, but here are a couple more ideas:

✓ Before anyone is allowed to vote, they have to pass a simple test to demonstrate they understand what they are voting for and what the expected outcomes are.

✓ Any politician that lobbies for votes by making false and misleading statements that even a complete idiot would see through should be stripped of office, have their assets seized and be made to work in voluntary service for the rest of their life.

Cameron snuck out of the back door, tail between his legs, never to be heard of again. Farage has almost gone to ground (I reckon he's either in Moscow or at Chez Trump's Mar-A-Logo) and Boris Johnson found a 'get out of jail free' card – initially due to the world being plunged into a Covid crisis, then via the antics of the despicable Moscow megalomaniac Putin. It's such a pity because if the world were still meandering along on an even keel, then the absurdity of leaving the trading block would be there for all to see – and undeniable.

On a more personal level, Brexit really impacted us in respect to Tenerife because once we were past the transition period, we would be unable to stay for more than three months during any six-month period. So that effectively meant our five-month stays were knocked on the head.

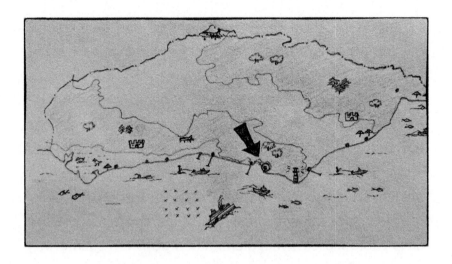

23 - REASONS TO BE CHEERFUL (PART 1)

Life was treating us well, perhaps as well as I had ever experienced. Certainly, I was more happy than I remember for an awfully long time and the main reason for me feeling like that was Judy. We had our ups and downs, of course, but it was spooky how closely aligned we were on so many things. I was cruising along with no stresses of any kind.

In mid-2015 I decided we should put together another short family getaway and I initiated 'Fam A Lam 2' – a long weekend in Nice in September for the children and their respective other halves. We would treat them – and that made us feel good.

Fran, who was now studying translation and business at Cardiff, didn't have a significant other at the time, so brought along her friend, the very charming and fun, Lottie. Steph, who was also studying Spanish and business at Manchester, but didn't like it there so was switching to Aberdeen, brought along her new boyfriend Blair, who coincidentally lived in Aberdeen! Ian was now with Jennica and recently settled in Sweden and John was with his then-girlfriend Chantelle. I knew my way round Nice enough to be able to book us a nice boutique hotel in a central location and I also made reservations at three very nice restaurants. The agenda had us spending one day in Nice, one in Monte Carlo and one in Cannes.

Naturally the weekend was boozy, but we covered a lot of ground too, mostly between bars and various eating places. I was excited to show them Monte Carlo and we walked the Grand Prix circuit and I bored the pants off them telling them how it all worked and recalling lots of stories from my now three visits to the Grand Prix.

Our last visit to the Monaco Grand Prix was in 2014, when we went with Giles and Linda. We did it in some style, with grandstand seats behind the swimming pool so we could see the cars exiting the tunnel and head right past us to the last corner before the pits. We were blessed with fabulous weather and on race day we packed up a couple of huge cold bags, made an enormous picnic and managed to haul it all on the train from the other side of Nice and then down through the streets of Monte Carlo (the station sits right at the top of the town) to our seats. If I remember correctly we had four wine boxes, so about nine litres of wine. Thankfully, we ended up sharing some of it with others sat nearby but, even so, Judy said it was the most drunk she had ever seen me, which was odd as I said the very same about her!

I gave everyone €100 each and we hit the casino. Steph, who does like a gamble, was straight at it and lost the lot before others had even started! Obviously it's not your run of the mill casino and can be quite intimidating, so I helped them settle. Suffice to say, less than an hour later when we left the casino, they were €1,000 better off.

By late 2015, Judy's knees were giving her major problems, the left one particularly. She had damaged them pretty badly at school and in the years following, as a result of playing netball in an era when sports science had hardly even been considered, let alone practised. She was playing on rock hard courts with shoes that provided little protection. She'd had the knee cartilage scraped a few times (arthoroscopies), but it required more industrial attention to properly fix it. Simultaneously, I was getting a bit fed up sitting at home working – or not working – alone and Judy was tiring of her job, too. Not only was she required to visit the Manchester call centre more regularly – which was a drag of epic proportions – but her mother had suffered bouts of quite serious illness and required recurring hospital visits. Unfortunately, her deeply unimpressive and unsympathetic boss showed virtually zero consideration for her situation when she sought some flexibility around her work hours. So, after a good deal of discussion, we decided that she would get her knee fixed permanently, which meant a replacement and a considerable period of time off work as it recovered. She went to see a specialist with the inevitable outcome. By now, she had pretty well given up on work such was the attitude of her (still) deeply unimpressive boss and she got herself signed off sick with the oft-used 'stress' card. I should add here that, in the 20 years of working, Judy had no more than six days of absence, which included 10 years bringing her boys up alone. She was, hitherto, loyal and diligent in the extreme.

We visited the hospital in the spring of 2016, a few days before the operation for a group session with all knee replacement patients due to be operated on that week. The session was led by the surgeon who explained a few things: preparation; the procedure and after care. Two things struck me. Firstly, the number of people in the room – clearly most had other halves with them but there were still about 15 or so people there who would be operated on and, given that the operation was five or six hours, it was clear that this was all the bloke did. I thought it must be a bit tedious – well, very tedious – and I found myself wondering if his mind ever began to stray during a procedure! Anyway, at about £8,000 a time I could understand how he was able to run the new Porsche Carrera that was sat outside the front door of Gatwick Park Hospital! Fifteen multiplied by £8,000 (less costs) is a fairly hefty number. The second thing of note was the replacement knee that was passed around, so we could examine what was going in. In 2016, I was expecting some high-tech material – polycarbonate or similar. What we were given was far from it! As it was passed to me, I dropped it, totally unprepared for the weight. If it had hit my foot I think it would have broken a toe! I can only hazard a guess but it was around 4lbs (2kg) of solid steel – so much for technology.

On the day of the operation, we were sat in a room together and about 45 minutes before going for the anaesthetic a nurse came in to prepare Judy. Basically she told Judy to change into a surgical gown and gave her a quick run down of what would happen, with an emphasis on the post-surgery bit, as she came round from the anaesthetic. I thought it was totally unnecessary for her to say: "I'll be honest, this is one of the most painful operations you can have." Judy was obviously nervous enough, but I saw the colour drain from her face and I felt for her and wished I could swap places.

As it happened, Judy coped remarkably well with the after effects of the operation – she is nothing but stoic and very brave. She didn't complain and was diligent in following her quite tough exercise regime to make sure the new knee settled in and worked well – and it did.

We had already decided that she wouldn't return to work again. She had, until that point, had a good relationship with her boss and she was the most dependable of his team. The other members were a mixed group of varying ability, most of whom had found their way into HR via other functions. Therefore, Judy had hoped her boss might recognise her value and loyalty and set up a decent redundancy, but no, there was nothing of the sort. So she waited until she clocked over 20 years of service – thus enabling her to get 20 years of flight benefits for both of us on British Airways – and then quit on the day her certificate of absence for the knee replacement expired. It was the end of an era for her and the start of an era for us.

We had been planning for her departure from work for several months and part of that plan was moving from Horsham, because there was now no reason to live there. As nice as Horsham was, it was still a commuter town, with a vast amount of building going on all over the place. It was not only beginning to feel very crowded but it was rapidly joining up with Crawley, which we didn't think would do it any favours.

Judy liked the idea of being by the sea, but we didn't really know where to look. We decided to take a couple of days and we drove down to Worthing and then headed east along the coast all the way to Rye, stopping at most towns along the way and staying overnight somewhere en route. We missed out Brighton and Hove – we both love it there, but house prices were too high and we didn't want the big city environment.

With no disrespect intended to any of the residents of these places (we all have our different views and I respect that, but...) we ruled out Worthing and most of the area between there and Brighton for one simple reason – the A27. How on earth anyone can put up with that road, which has to be used to get anywhere, is beyond me. To the east of Brighton, the area from Saltdean to Newhaven is OK but appears to have been planned out by a 5 year old, it really is a mish mash of housing and again suffers with the consequences of one road (the coastal A259) Then you hit Newhaven which has such high potential due to the location but is badly in need of regeneration and just too industrial for us. Further along Seaford, then Eastbourne before getting to Bexhill, Hastings and Rye. Rye is so far out on a limb it's scary – the thought of living the rest of our lives in isolation didn't appeal. Scary for different reasons were Bexhill and Hastings, not so much about regeneration, but there was just an atmosphere about those places that felt quite uncomfortable to us. For some inexplicable reason, neither of us felt particularly safe although we couldn't really put our finger on it. Easier to identify was that we were still out on a limb and so far from anywhere – road links weren't good and rail not much better. So we narrowed our search down to Eastbourne – specifically the west side around Bede's school – and Seaford. We decided to go wherever we could find the right house. Having viewed several in both places, we eventually found the ideal one in Seaford in a nice part of town on the south east side.

Selling Horsham was predictably easy – the agent didn't even get to produce any particulars. He visited us one morning, we had a viewing that afternoon and were offered our asking price (more than we expected) the next afternoon. The buyer was ready to go.

The house move went very simply and seamlessly and so began yet another exciting chapter in my/our lives. We were both looking forward with a huge amount of optimism.

24 - LUCKY 13

I was 62 when I moved into the 13th house I've owned and I was determined to make it the last. I told my girls that if I ever suggest moving again, they should shoot me. Just like many of the other houses, it was nice - but in need of some work. Downstairs was a reasonable size thanks to a full-width ground floor extension, but upstairs was too small. So we soon set about extending the rear bedroom to make a much larger main bedroom with en-suite. That bedroom faced due south, as did the kitchen and dining room, which was ideal - I wasn't making the same mistake as Horsham. The garden was of a size that allowed Judy to get her teeth stuck into - not too large that it was overwhelming, but big enough to give her plenty to occupy her time. Judy is passionate about gardening and she will happily spend hours tending to and moving plants from one spot to another

... and back again!

Our neighbours were all lovely and it was a very nice touch that Dave and Viv next door gathered other nearby neighbours together for us to be properly introduced.

We're only a stone's throw from the sea – and there are plenty of stones there – and there's something quite enchanting about being so close to it. Neither of us can really describe it, but it never loses its appeal and, on a sunny and calm day, it can be so peaceful and stimulating. The countryside around us is about as spectacular as I have come across in this country. Granted, it's not Snowdonia or The Lake District, but it is very beautiful and, in places, very dramatic. We get our fair share of tourists in Seaford, particularly Japanese as the view across Cuckmere Haven and the Coastguard Cottages (regularly seen in TV and movie scenes) is iconic to them. I heard somewhere it is the most popular screensaver in Japan, although I'm not sure whether I believe that ...

We settled in to Seaford life quickly. Judy had to give three month's notice and, thankfully, they allowed her to simply work a day or two handing over and then she was gone. It didn't take too long to adjust because she had hardly worked for the preceding four months, due to her operation.

In June 2016, Fran graduated from Cardiff University, she had done well and I was the typical proud father when she went up on stage to collect her certificate.

That said, I was never that enthusiastic about either of the girls going to university and I talked to them both about that in their teens. I wasn't trying to dissuade them - as I knew they would go - but I wanted them to understand where the value in getting a degree lay. It wasn't going to make them smarter, it wouldn't elevate them to a superior level, nor would (a general degree course) particularly help them in their career. I told them to make the very most of all of the social aspects of university because that would be the greatest benefit they could take from it and something that would sustain through life. I stand by that thinking today. What I was really pleased about with both my girls was that university sandwiched some really valuable life experience activities, which I think has put them in a great position to deal with the challenges of life. Both have travelled extensively and have survived the Asia backpacking experience. Fran (with partner Ben) also travelled for many months around Australia (including the outback) and they spent a ski season in Val d'Isere as chalet hosts, with more than a fair share of interesting experiences. In addition to the long-distance travels, Steph spent six months in Barcelona, supposedly learning the language except she didn't really, as all the Spaniards wanted to speak to her in English so they could improve their skills! She has since moved out to Australia where she has now been for nearly three years and has managed to look after herself well and prosper. It is these things that I am most proud about (so far) and both Fran and Steph have learned so much from their experiences. I like to take some credit for bringing them both up with my 'prepared to have a go at anything' attitude. Not only that, but they've learned how to deal with life independently.

In summer 2016 our life is all but perfect. Judy spends a lot of time in the garden and I joined the golf club - a good course only about a mile away - and got in with a good group of golfers. My work didn't demand very much of me at all and I was able to manage my hours easily to fit in with our social activities.

We headed off to Tenerife in late October and I occupied my time there with a mixture of my work and managing the agents for the community. By now, I had assigned Judy the job of managing the gardens and our gardener. She really enjoyed it, but was never really able to get the gardener out of first gear, she was too nice to him! Regardless of that, she was able to put the effort in herself and made the gardens beautiful, introducing all kinds of plants. It's probably fair to say I was the most content I have ever been - and thoroughly enjoying life.

As you might imagine, given how she treats everyone else in life, Judy was a very attentive and caring daughter. Her father died when she was quite young, but she visited her mum, Margaret, who was then 97 and under the care of her brother Peter, frequently in her house in Crawley. In early 2017 her mum eventually succumbed to the inevitable and we moved her into a delightful nursing home in the Sussex countryside, between Lewes and Haywards Heath. Judy had been anxious about her mum's welfare and this move relieved her of those worries.

Clearing her house was a nightmare – I discovered she was a hoarder, although most people are by comparison to me! I took over the role of looking after her finances – she didn't have a huge amount, but the proceeds from the house sale ensured she could live in comfort for the rest of her days, which she did. Margaret eventually passed away peacefully in 2020 at the grand age of 101.

We bumbled along on a very nice path, splitting our time between Seaford and Tenerife and dodging winters almost completely. Stephanie graduated from Aberdeen University in June 2018 and a few months later – in August – Ian and Jennica got married in Sweden. They chose an old castle as the venue near where Jennica grew up in southern Sweden, not too far from Malmo. I knew the Swedes were capable drinkers but I wasn't prepared for downing schnapps on the coach to the venue at 10.00 in the morning! It was a lovely, open air event and very, very boozy. As I recall, the best man was unable to deliver his speech such was the volume he had drunk. We got back to our house at about 2.00 in the morning, 16 hours after we left – and definitely much worse for wear.

Earlier in 2018, I had dipped my toe in the crypto-currency water, even though I was not convinced (and I'm still not). But I put £3,000 into 'Ripple' and in a matter of only a few weeks, had turned a near £20,000 profit. Having had enough experience of investment gains and losses – and still not really believing in the whole crypto thing – I cashed out and used the money to fund 'Fam a Lam 3'. I needed to go one better than Nice and – helped by the crypto cash – it wasn't difficult.

Inevitably, I chose Vegas and spent many thoroughly enjoyable hours putting together a most comprehensive itinerary. We actually flew to LA – because I got such a good deal with Norwegian – and then hired two people carriers, which Judy and I drove the four hours across the desert. The first item on the itinerary was to stop at Barstow (a large town with absolutely no purpose) in the middle of the Mojave desert, so that everyone could sample the delights of In and Out burger. The food was a resounding success and set the tone for what was to follow. During the week, I had booked a restaurant for every evening, a Cirque Du Soleil show, twilight helicopter trips taking in the spectacle of the strip and a variety of other activities that filled our days and nights. We stayed on the strip at the MGM Signature and I gave everyone $500 each so they could have fun in the casinos, which they did. At the end of the week, we headed into LA and I showed them the craziness of Venice Beach and then we had lunch at a delightful restaurant in Santa Monica before boarding our flight home. The trip was a great success and one that I reflect on often. I regret not having done more 'Fam a Lam' trips, although goodness knows when we would have fitted them in!

After Vegas, Judy and I were only back in Seaford for a few days before we headed out to Tenerife. Our neighbour Dave did a grand job of keeping an eye on the house while we were away - he picked up the mail and went in every week to make sure we hadn't sprung a leak or experienced any other kind of disaster. In return, we gave him our season tickets at the Amex and he became a regular at home matches.

The club got promoted to the Premier League in 2017 and it was only the second time in my lifetime that they had played in the top division - a brilliant achievement! If I'm honest, I didn't expect us to last more than one season there, so I intended to make the most of every minute of it, such that I could anyway. My fears around longevity in the division were 'rubber stamped' in our very first game when we played Manchester City at home. I think the entire game was played in our penalty box, with Brighton hoofing balls out to the halfway line, one of their players would go back and collect it and then they would stand on the edge of our box trying to fathom how to get it from there and into the goal. Think 'Siege of Alamo', but worse. I'll make no apology that I knew there and then that we needed a more adventurous manager than Chris Hughton, maybe not immediately but most certainly we needed someone with a bit more ambition and inventiveness if the club were to survive and progress. That wasn't a view held by a large proportion of fans who had come to regard Hughton as something of a hero, so I kept quiet on that subject when the forum went into overdrive. How we only lost that game 0-2 is still a mystery.

As would be the norm for the time of year we were in Tenerife in February 2019 when neighbour Dave phoned telling us we had been burgled. Thankfully they hadn't trashed the house, but some of the contents of wardrobes were scattered around the floor. The timing was awful as I was chairing the community AGM a few days later. Judy definitely needed to go back as it was her jewellery that was likely to be gone. I had very little of any interest to a burglar in the house – anything of value I had with me. So Judy went back on her own and discovered that she had lost about five pieces of jewellery with a collective value of about £3,000 – my camera (worth about £500) was also gone. While Judy was still in Seaford, I had some security devices installed on the recommendation of the crime prevention officer (camera and lights all activated by phone) and, later, an alarm installed. Judy returned to Tenerife within a week – it could've been much worse than it was.

We put in the insurance claim for £3,500 and Judy was very thorough when describing the detail of the jewellery. A week later I got a call from a Hatton Garden jeweller telling me the information had been passed to him and he would like to visit us at home with his products so that Judy could pick replacements. I told him that not only were we away, but that the items were rarely, if ever, worn (they were purely sentimental) and we might not want to replace them. He said it was perfectly OK to pick other items and they didn't need to be like-for-like. He was quite persistent but I really couldn't be bothered listening to him, so I told him I would call him again when we returned home. Judy and I talked about it and she said she didn't really want anything replaced – all the jewellery she ever wore was with us in Tenerife. So I phoned the insurance company, told them about the annoying man from the jewellers and added that we didn't really want to replace the items stolen so could we just be paid for the claim? He said that was fine and that he would authorise the payment there and then. He put me on hold momentarily and came back saying he had just made a bank payment of £7,377 to us. I was taken aback and asked him how he had arrived at such a figure. He told me it was due to the fact that they send the description of the items to their contracted jeweller in order to get an accurate valuation and that was the figure the jeweller arrived at. Note to self: in a future life, come back either as a jeweller (money for old rope) or CEO of a general insurance business (put an end to such fraud).

Judy is the most wonderful cook and can turn her hand to just about anything. I thought I would surprise her by entering her into Masterchef without telling her! Completing the application was a major challenge as it was very detailed and it took me a few weeks of casually asking Judy scores of questions to get all the answers I needed. I submitted the application not expecting to hear anything but a few weeks later I got an email (I used my email address, not hers) saying I (Judy) had been selected for a phone audition. I now had to own up and whilst she wasn't best pleased she did warm to the idea. She sailed through three phone interviews and was then selected for an in-person audition at the studios in East London.

Judy had to prepare a dish in advance, take it with her and then assemble it when she got there. She makes a spectacular Nasi Goreng and decided to do that. When we got to the studios, she was one of the last contestants of the day and the judges' assistant warned her that they had eaten a huge amount during the day and not to be concerned if they just picked at her dish. She put it together and went into a room with the three judges who not only tried her food but gave her a bit of a grilling to better understand her and her general food knowledge. Judy came out about half an hour later saying she wasn't sure how it went, but that they had eaten every last bit of the food she made. I knew then that she'd been successful. Sure enough, about a week later she got a call telling her she had made the finals and would be appearing in heat three in the late autumn.

When the date eventually came around, Judy was much calmer than I expected and took it all in her stride. She had to stay over the night before as they were required to be at the studios by 08.00 and they didn't actually get away until well after 18.00. Much of the day was preparation, taking them through how it would all run and then make up. They didn't actually get into the kitchen until the early afternoon. I'd love to tell you what happened but Judy was required to sign an NDA (non-disclosure agreement) and she is still bothered by it to this day. Suffice to say what you see on TV isn't the way it happened on the day. For example, they started cooking at around 14.00 and didn't leave the kitchen until well after 17.00. There were several takes and retakes. Judy didn't make it to the next round and I will say, without fear of contradiction, that it was nothing to do with her cooking. While I am quite sure she wouldn't have won the competition, I am equally sure her food was good enough for her to progress to the next round at the very least.

That said, she had a wonderful time and it was a great experience for her. She should be proud that from more than 6,000 applicants, she made it down to the final TV stages.

Another big moment for Judy in 2019 was when she became a Grandma, to Alfie – Ian and Jennica's first son. Another grandchild followed in December 2021, when Alfie's brother, Louis, was born. Judy will be a brilliant Grandma – it's a pity the family is so far away, but she will figure that one out I have no doubt.

Judy's Mum passed away in mid-2020 and the funeral service was held at the crematorium in Crawley. The undertakers had recommended a vicar from a church in Lindfield to lead the simple service and Judy had one or two conversations over the phone in the days leading up to the funeral in order that he could be familiarised and prepared. I haven't been to many funerals, but Stuart Silk led a most intimate and almost uplifting service. He was compassionate and thought-provoking – and both Judy and I instantly warmed to him. We talked with him afterwards and have been to see him several times since, attending his Sunday services.

I've tried to understand a little more about the church and the faith, but I struggle with it for many reasons. I have a real need to try and believe but there are so many contradictions that I doubt if I ever will. Judy puts it so well though, it might be difficult to believe but we should understand and practice the values that are promoted through the bible. She is absolutely correct of course and, although it's a bit late now, I am at least trying.

December 2020, and the end of an era when my boss called me to tell me the company was laying off all independent contractors, due to the highly restrictive tax regime known as IR35 and so my work needs wrapping up. It was a pity, but I'd had a very good five years with the business – the only surprise was that it lasted so long! I would now officially retire.

That call came when we were in Tenerife, we had become stranded there due to the Covid pandemic and there simply weren't any flights home, so we spent that Christmas there along with Judy's sister Dorothy who had taken a seasonal rental nearby. We managed to enjoy ourselves – and having a Christmas away from home in the sun surely beat what was going on at home, with most people locked down. We eventually came home in March 2021 after nearly six months away.

A combination of Brexit, (by this time, we were at the end of the transition phase) and my upcoming diagnosis, led us to reluctantly put our Tenerife home on the market. The process was painful and the agent was absolutely hopeless. I was forced to write the particulars myself and had to pretty much tell them how to take the photos. After seven months we'd got nowhere so another agent stepped in (we had to pay two lots of 3% commission). They sold it to a Ukrainian in one of the dodgiest financial transactions I have ever been involved in - so much so that I am scared to say any more about it. Dave was really very good about the division of proceeds and if I had any worries about that before, they were clearly misplaced.

Apart from being a very frequent visitor to Eastbourne Hospital for chemotherapy and immunotherapy - as well as the odd A&E visit - we spent most of 2022 travelling and sightseeing. Although my insurance restricted me to European travel only, Judy and I visited some wonderful places and friends joined us to share these most special and precious time. I've been trying to burn through 25 years of holiday and social budgets in a little over a year - and I think I've done a pretty good job of it!

Another thing I've done a good job at is getting Judy into golf, which I achieved in early 2022. I figured it would help build a network of friends locally, rather than the ones we have dotted all over the country. In typical Judy fashion, she really grasped the bull by the horns and very quickly became quite the capable golfer. She hits the ball a long way and once she sorts out her dreadful putting she will break 100 with ease! She is very enthusiastic about golf and I am thrilled for her and she should be very proud of what she has achieved in such a short time. The highlight of her golf so far has to be a trip we went on to the Algarve in October 2021 with Burchett and Kevin, who now lives there. We played three days of four-ball golf, put on our standard bets and Judy won on the first day and pocketed a well-deserved €80. Well done Judy! My one regret, I suppose, is that we didn't do this 15 or so years ago. I have no doubt that within two years she will be one of the best lady golfers at the club, probably on a committee and maybe even the captain a year or to later. I'm so very happy for her.

25 - I HEAR YOU KNOCKING

Christmas 2022 and I have had the news from my Oncologist that my immunotherapy isn't working and that the cancer has returned. I'm waiting to hear what happens next, the most likely thing is that the treatment will just be stopped as it's ineffective; but I'm a gambler and so maybe there's one more roll of the dice. Anyway I'm far too busy to go and meet my maker right now. We've a trip to Tenerife planned and another golf trip to the Algarve with Adz and Emma shortly after and most importantly, Fran and Ben are getting married in May. I was realistic enough not to plan too far ahead and I've even organised a golf trip for Judy and some of her new found golf club pals to go back to The Algarve in November. She desperately wanted to hold a place open for me but I convinced her it was futile.

I've used the past year to teach Judy all my jobs and

she can now (just about) manage all the finances, all the bills are now in her name, she can change water filters and put salt into the water softener and even knows when and how to sharpen the lawnmower blades. For those things that I think she might struggle with I have told her which of my friends to go to. There's nothing really left for me to do!

We've had a lovely Christmas with Fran, Steph and Ben. Unfortunately Ian, Jennica and boys couldn't make it, they were with Ian's dad up in Preston and the inconsiderate railway workers who are on strike put paid to us seeing them.

New Years Eve and we have Phil and Ceris and Stewart and Ellen coming over, we're going to watch Brighton play Arsenal and then we have a Thai banquet lined up courtesy of Judy and which I know will be brilliant.

I started writing this book in January of this year (2022) and said that I wanted it complete by the end of the year. It's now 11.15am on December 31st so I'm going to wrap up and meet my target with 12 or so hours spare, I never miss deadlines!

I look back with an immense sense of pride at what I have accomplished, but also some regrets for my failings and for which I have sought forgiveness. If ever the term 'experiential learning' applied to anyone then that's me, and another well used term, 'better late than never' equally applies I think/hope.

Of the things I am most proud of they are my two children who I naturally worry for, as they still have lots to learn, but they have turned out as well as I could have hoped, and I take my share of credit for that. Although I was the absent parent for much of their childhood I worked tirelessly to give them the benefit of my experience, keep them on the straight and narrow and help them develop as best I could. Thankfully, they had an attentive and caring Mum, which made my job all the easier.

I am also proud to have met and been able to spend the last years of my life with someone as special as Judy. Someone once told me I was punching above my weight, blimey what an understatement, I have been privileged, nothing less. In many ways we are chalk and cheese but our relative strengths complimented each other so well. We had our moments of course but 'we rocked on well' (a Judyism). I will miss her so very much, my light, my soul and my reason for pretty well everything.

Over the past months I have tried to rationalise what lies beyond, in particular the validity of eternal life that the Church tells us about. I know I'm not there but I sense there's something, that is my hope and that it will facilitate my being able to reunite with all those that have made my life so very happy and fulfilling, and give me the opportunity to put right the few things that I will leave undone.

I hope you have enjoyed my account, the ups, downs, happiness and sadness. I set out to make it a fun read and I know it has morphed into something else, but in doing so I hope it hasn't detracted from entertaining you.

The legend that is Frank Sinatra put it so well in his trademark song:

And now, the end is near
    And so I face the final curtain
    My friends, I'll say it clear
    I'll state my case of which I'm certain
    I've lived a life that's full
    I travelled each and every highway
    But more, much more than this
    I did it my way
Regrets, I've had a few
    But then again, too few to mention
    I did what I had to do
    And saw it through without exemption
    I planned each chartered course
    Each careful step along the byway
    But more, much more than this
    I did it my way
For what is a man, what has he got
    If not himself then he has not
    To say all the things he truly feels
    And not the words of one who kneels
    The record shows, I took the blows
    But I did it my way

Hang on, there's a knock at the door, I wonder who's calling?

Au revoir

When in distress to Him I called
He to my rescue came

Printed in Great Britain
by Amazon

20172764R00188